DELiverance
— MADE EASY —

DELIVERANCE
— MADE EASY —

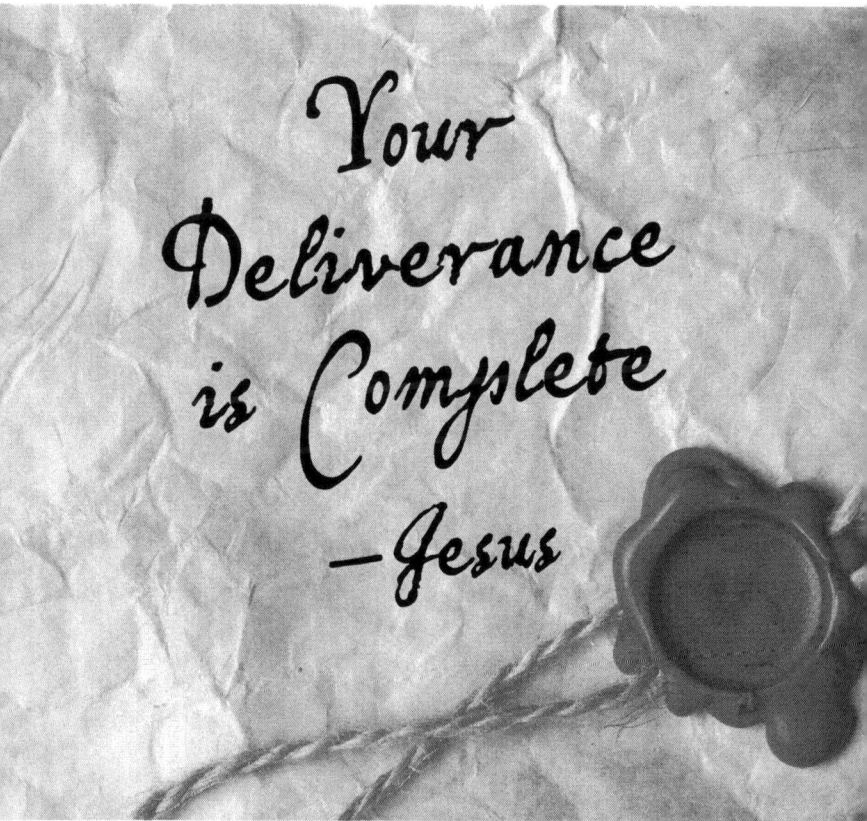

Your Deliverance is Complete

—Jesus

DR. KEVIN L. ZADAI

trademarks registered in the United States Patent and Trademark Office by Biblica, Inc.™

Scripture quotations marked (AMP) are taken from the Amplified Bible, Copyright © 1954, 1958, 1962, 1964, 1965, 1987 by The Lockman Foundation. Used by permission. www. Lockman.org. (The AMP regularly uses parentheses and brackets throughout. Unless otherwise noted, these are in the original and were not added by the author.)

Please note that Warrior Notes publishing style capitalizes certain pronouns in Scripture that refer to the Father, Son, and Holy Spirit, which may differ from some publishers' styles. Take note that the name "satan" and related names are not capitalized. We choose not to acknowledge him, even to the point of violating accepted grammatical rules. The author and Warrior Notes have made an intentional decision to italicize many Scriptures in block quotes.

Warrior Notes Publishing
P O Box 1288
Destrehan, LA 70047

Cover design: Virtually Possible Designs

For more information about our school, go to www.warriornotesschool.com. Reach us on the internet: www.Kevinzadai.com

ISBN 13 TP: 978-1-6631-0076-4

ISBN 13 eBook: 978-1-6631-0077-1

ISBN 13 Audiobook: 978-1-6631-0078-8

DEDICATION

I dedicate this book to the Lord Jesus Christ. When I died during surgery and met with Jesus on the other side, He insisted that I return to life on earth and help people with their destinies. Because of Jesus's love and concern for people, the Lord has actually chosen to send a person back from death to help everyone who will receive that help so that their destiny and purpose are secure in Him.

I want You, Lord, to know that when You come to take me to be with You someday, I sincerely hope that people remember not me but the revelation of Jesus Christ that You have revealed through me. I want others to know that I am merely being obedient to my heavenly calling and mission, which is to reveal Your plan to fulfill the divine destiny for each of God's children.

ACKNOWLEDGMENTS

In addition to sharing my story with everyone through the book *Heavenly Visitation: A Guide to the Supernatural,* God has commissioned me to write over sixty books and study guides. Most recently, the Lord gave me the commission to produce this book, *Deliverance Made Easy.* This book addresses some of the revelations concerning the areas that Jesus revealed to me through the Word of God and by the Spirit of God during several visitations. I want to thank everyone who has encouraged, assisted, and prayed for me while writing this work. Special thanks to my wonderful wife, Kathi, for her love and dedication to the Lord and me. Thank you to my excellent staff for the beautiful job editing this book. Special thanks as well to all my friends who understand that deliverance has been made easy. You are ready for the next move of God's Spirit!

CONTENTS

Introduction 13

Chapter 1   The Origin of Spiritual Warfare 15

Chapter 2   The Enemy's Covert Operation 29

Chapter 3   Parameters of Spiritual Authority 41

Chapter 4   The Battle for Your Mind 55

Chapter 5   The Truth Sets Captives Free 71

Chapter 6   Old Testament Framework for Deliverance . . . 87

Chapter 7   Jesus Paid for Your Freedom 99

Chapter 8   The Battle Is Already Won 113

Chapter 9   The Lord's Angelic Army 127

Chapter 10   God Is Your Deliverer 141

Salvation Prayer 157

About Dr. Kevin Zadai 159

INTRODUCTION

Many modern-day ministries have complicated the subject of deliverance. Yet the truth is that it is very simple once we understand what we are contending with. With the authority given through Jesus Christ, every believer is called to walk in permanent freedom and minister to others. Deliverance was never intended to be a specialized ministry for the spiritually elite, but it should be our lifestyle in the body of Christ.

In this book, we will explore Scriptures that reveal how spiritual warfare originated, the victory that has already been won, and how to daily deal with the enemy in every situation you encounter. I pray that you become well-versed in this topic and see powerful results in your life. As you receive the revelation that deliverance is easy, I believe you will also help set many people free and teach them to understand our spiritual battle.

Blessings,

Dr. Kevin L. Zadai

CHAPTER 1

THE ORIGIN OF SPIRITUAL WARFARE

And He said to them, "I saw satan fall like lightning from heaven. Behold, I give you the authority to trample on serpents and scorpions, and over all the power of the enemy, and nothing shall by any means hurt you."

—Luke 10:18–19

The Lord instructed me to write this book to bring understanding of the dynamics of deliverance. Many people do not understand how demons operate both in the lives of believers and nonbelievers. Although I will give a brief overview of the history of satan and the origins of demons, that will not be the focus of this work. This writing aims to equip you to practically execute victory over the unseen enemy you deal with daily. Just as Jesus and His disciples drove out demons, every believer is called to operate in deliverance.

As far as scholars know, satan was a guardian cherub in the Garden of Eden (Ezekiel 28:13–19). We will not go into detail about his origin; the focus will be on how spiritual warfare became an issue with people. The battle started in the garden (Genesis 3); then Genesis

6 shows us what happened afterward. Understanding how the enemy operates behind the scenes is crucial when dealing with daily situations.

The body of Christ struggles with an overwhelming misunderstanding concerning the operation of demonic spirits. I will highlight specific Scriptures to reveal some truths you may not know. Demons are fallen hybrid spirits who are evil, stubborn, and covert. They do not like to be obvious because if exposed, you can effectively deal with them so that they can no longer operate. So they are careful not to reveal their position unless they have to. If you are a threat to them, you may have experiences that others will not.

SONS OF GOD AND DAUGHTERS OF MEN

Now it came to pass, when men began to multiply on the face of the earth, and daughters were born to them, that the sons of God saw the daughters of men, that they were beautiful; and they took wives for themselves of all whom they chose.

—Genesis 6:1–2

Genesis 6 is one of my favorite yet one of the most misunderstood chapters in the Bible, but after this study, I hope you will have a better grasp of it. As we delve into this passage, I must note that Moses is the author of Genesis. Interestingly, the Genesis events did not occur while Moses was alive. That is pretty peculiar. All the Hebrew scholars, rabbis, and even Jewish traditions say that Moses wrote Genesis. It was given to him on the mountain of God; therefore, the entire book is supernatural. We must understand that he wrote it out as it was dictated to him. With that said, the specific wording, phrases, and order is there for a reason. We must break it down, read every word—not every verse, every word—and group it into phrases.

Understanding how the enemy operates behind the scenes is crucial when dealing with daily situations.

Genesis 6:1 states that the people on the earth began to multiply, and daughters were born to them. The reason it starts this way is not only to describe the process of multiplication among human beings but to set up the chapter for the revelation of what else occurred. This passage speaks of daughters born to men; the following phrase describes different beings. The sons of God differ from daughters born to men or the people on earth. Notice that this verse does not say the sons of God began to multiply on the planet; it says that men or human beings began to multiply on the face of the earth. So the humans and the daughters born to them were one set of entities, and the sons of God were another distinct set.

The sons of God saw the beautiful women or the daughters of men, and they took any they wanted as their wives (Genesis 6:2). The problem was that the sons of God were giant hybrid races, like the ones in later times that Samson dealt with in Judges 14–16. The Jewish people, including Samson, were forbidden to marry anybody from other countries (Deuteronomy 7:3; Judges 14:3), especially from the Philistine camps known to have these hybrids. This interbreeding problem started during the period before the flood in Genesis and then crept up again afterward.

THE SERPENT'S SEED

The Lord God said to the serpent, "Because you have done this, you are cursed more than all the cattle, and more than any animal of the field; On your belly you shall go, and dust you shall eat all the days of your life. And I will put enmity (open hostility) between you and the woman, and between your seed (offspring) and her Seed; He shall [fatally] bruise your head, and you shall [only] bruise His heel."

—Genesis 3:14–15 AMP

The sons of God were the sons of Adam who lived for between eight and nine hundred years after the fall. The line of Adam's son Cain, who sinned by killing his brother Abel, bore the devil's offspring. (See Genesis 4.) This hybrid line infiltrated Cain's line and came through him. Genesis 3:15 prophesied that the serpent's offspring would bite and bruise the heel of the woman's offspring; this Scripture reveals what happened.

Cain rebelled against God; Hebrews 11:4 says that his brother Abel was righteous, and he was not. If you study the lineage of Cain, you will see the corruption that infiltrated his genealogy. Cain was cursed because he murdered his brother, and his offspring were the seed of the serpent. Of course, God never intended for Abel to be killed. The bottom line is that the sons of God interbred with the daughters of men, and at a certain point, God intervened.

> And the Lord said, "My Spirit shall not strive with man forever, for he is indeed flesh; yet his days shall be one hundred and twenty years."
>
> —Genesis 6:3

God was so upset with the wickedness of people that He limited their average lifespan to no more than 120 years (Genesis 6:3). God did not want interbreeding to occur nor did He want hybrid offspring to live longer because they were corrupt. Not everyone was evil then, but for the most part, the situation with humanity was terrible. God's Spirit would no longer strive with human beings, so He decided to curb their wickedness.

After Adam and Eve fell in the Garden of Eden, satan immediately went after the woman's seed. He tried to intercept the plan of God to send our deliverer, Jesus Christ. The devil knew that Jesus had to come through a pure human body, so he attempted to infiltrate humanity to thwart God's plan. If he could cause people to inter-breed so that they were no longer fully human but part animal or some other entity, then Jesus could not be the perfect sacrifice without blemish. He had to come through a genetically pure human line in order to redeem us.

The world became so corrupt that Noah and his family of eight were the only pure humans left. Only the eight people on the ark were perfect in their generations or genetically pure (Genesis 6:8–9). They were the only ones who did not allow the serpent's seed to corrupt their bloodlines. God destroyed the rest in the great flood of Noah's time (Genesis 7).

UNDERSTANDING THE NEPHILIM

> *The Nephilim were on the earth in those days, and also afterward, when the sons of God came in to the daughters of man and they bore chil-dren to them. These were the mighty men who were of old, the men of renown.*

> —Genesis 6:4 ESV

In addition to the sons of God and the daughters of men, Genesis 6:4 mentions another subset of entities. It says that in those days and for some time afterward, the Nephilim lived on the earth. Then, it explains that the sons of God had intercourse with the women who gave birth to children who became the heroes and famous warriors of ancient times. They crossed the boundary that God set.

> *And the angels who did not stay within their own position of authority, but left their proper dwelling, He has kept in eternal chains under gloomy darkness until the judgment of the great day—just as Sodom and Gomorrah and the surrounding cities, which likewise indulged in sexual immorality and pursued unnatural desire, serve as an example by undergoing a punishment of eternal fire.*
>
> —Jude 1:6–7 ESV

Jesus had to come through a genetically pure human line in order to redeem us.

> *For if God did not spare angels when they sinned, but cast them into hell and committed*

> *them to chains of gloomy darkness to be kept*
> *until the judgment.*

> —2 Peter 2:4 ESV

The Nephilim were the fallen angels that left their abode; according to Peter and Jude, they are now in chains. Since these fallen angels are chained, they cannot be demons that inhabit people. However, they taught people to sin by influencing the sons of God to go into the daughters of men, resulting in this interbreeding in Genesis 6.

As I previously mentioned, we must divide the entities in Genesis 6 into subsets to understand what took place. There are the sons of God, the daughters of men, and the Nephilim. They were the fallen angels that were with lucifer in the Garden of Eden. The root of the word Nephilim is napal, which means "to fall" or "be cast down."[1] The devil originally was a bright and shiny one, whose name was actually helel, according to Isaiah 14:12.[2] You can see that the Hebrew word there is not lucifer; it's the word helel, which means "the bright and shining one of God."

The Nephilim who left their abode, influenced people to sin and were not the ones who went into the

---

1. "H5307 - *nāp̄al* - Strong's Hebrew Lexicon," Blue Letter Bible, accessed June 30, 2023. https://www.blueletterbible.org/lexicon/h5307/esv/wlc/0-1/.
2. "H1966 - *hêlēl* - Strong's Hebrew Lexicon," Blue Letter Bible, accessed June 30, 2023. https://www.blueletterbible.org/lexicon/h1966/kjv/wlc/0-1/.

daughters of men. The Scripture states that the Nephilim were on earth in those days and the sons of God went into the daughters of men. Several things are going on here, which are sometimes confusing. But they cannot be interchanged. I wanted to thoroughly explain these verses because this is one of the most misunderstood topics in the Bible.

> *For when they rise from the dead, they neither marry nor are given in marriage, but are like angels in heaven.*
>
> —Mark 12:25

It does not surprise me that satan would create confusion about angels, demons, and spiritual warfare because he seeks to deceive and discredit believers. He wants you to believe and speak things that are not true. Angels cannot procreate. In Mark 12:25, Jesus clearly states that we will not have marriages when we get to Heaven—we will be like the angels. The angels do not get married because they are genderless although they can appear as men or women. God created these beings; they live beyond this realm and do not procreate. Nowhere in the Bible does it say that they can have children.

Angels cannot interbreed with human beings; however, they can cloak themselves and appear human. They have done that with all of us, and most of the time, we do not realize it. But to have children, you have to be a human being. So these truths in Genesis 6 have to be taken word for word, phrase by phrase, and put into subsets, as I call them. This will help you understand each of these groups.

> *But with the precious blood of Christ, as of a lamb without blemish and without spot.*
>
> —1 Peter 1:19

Due to the interbreeding between the sons of God and the daughters of men, these giant, fierce warriors were born. They had genetic defects, which is why the whole idea of a spotless lamb matters. "Without blemish and without spot" meant that there were no genetic defects. The genetic defects came because of interbreeding. You can see flaws in both animals and human beings today; this was never God's will.

HYBRID BEINGS AFTER THE FLOOD

> *Cush fathered Nimrod; he was the first on earth to be a mighty man. He was a mighty hunter before the Lord. Therefore it is said, "Like Nimrod a mighty hunter before the Lord." The beginning of his kingdom was Babel, Erech, Accad, and Calneh, in the land of Shinar.*
>
> —Genesis 10:8–10 ESV

In Greek mythology, there are many so-called gods, which you may have read about or seen portrayed in paintings. I have investigated some of the art from the walls of Babylon that Nimrod built and have reason to believe that hybrids may have inspired these images. Genesis 10:8 says that Nimrod was a mighty one who was one of the hybrids.

Before the flood, hybrid beings built the pyramids and other structures that we cannot even construct today. Then Nimrod, after the flood, began to restart that by building the Tower of Babel, so God had to come down and stop him (Genesis 11:1–9). Nimrod, who was known as the first architect, was deified and became known as Gilgamesh, which is where the mystical Mystery Babylon in Revelation 17 originated from.

To summarize, a whole race on earth had interbred before the flood; they were all hybrids except for Noah's family. Remember, only eight people made it onto the ark. Out of millions of people on earth, only eight were pure. God used their pure genealogy to preserve the lineage of the Messiah through the flood.

We see the giant races pop up again because genetic material was brought across the flood, which again infiltrated the human race. This is addressed through Noah, who said, "Cursed be Canaan" (Genesis 9:25); there is your clue. Genetic corruption occurred before and after the flood, allowing the giant races to return. Joshua and David were used as mighty warriors to defeat the giant races (Numbers 13:28–33; Joshua 11:21–23; 2 Samuel

5:17–25). When Israel entered the promised land and started to inhabit it, they drove out all these races and eventually extinguished the hybrid giants.

DISEMBODIED SPIRITS

The Lord saw that the wickedness of man was great in the earth, and that every intention of the thoughts of his was only evil continually. And the Lord regretted that he had made man on the earth, and it grieved him to his heart. So the Lord said, "I will blot out man whom I have created from the face of the land, man and animals and creeping things and birds of the heavens, for I am sorry that I have made them."

—Genesis 6:4–7 ESV

The Lord saw that the wickedness on earth was so evil that He destroyed all the human hybrids and animals in the floods except for the ones that He chose to be on the ark. God's heart was grieved, and He was sorry that He had made man and put them on earth. He decided to wipe out the human race He created from the face of the planet. Their bodies were destroyed, which caused their spirits to become disembodied. We now deal with these demons today. Not only did God destroy the people, but He also destroyed large and small animals and even birds. But Noah found favor in the sight of the

Lord because he had kept himself and his family pure (Genesis 6:8–9).

Spiritual warfare started in the Garden of Eden with helel deceiving Adam and Eve so that their eyes were opened to good and evil so that he could have his way with them (Genesis 3:1–7). Once he deceived them and they ate, they knew the difference between good and evil. Human beings did not previously know evil because only God could handle it. After they ate the fruit, they were cursed and driven out of the garden (Genesis 3:17–24). Instead of living forever, they now had a limited lifespan. People then started fighting disease, sin, and the results of the fall of man, leading us to where we are today.

> *Now there was a man in their synagogue with an unclean spirit. And he cried out, saying, "Let us alone! What have we to do with You, Jesus of Nazareth? Did You come to destroy us? I know who You are—the Holy One of God!"*
>
> *But Jesus rebuked him, saying, "Be quiet, and come out of him!" And when the unclean spirit had convulsed him and cried out with a loud voice, he came of out him.*
>
> —Mark 1:23–26

As mentioned, we can see in the Bible that the fallen angels are all chained. Notice that when Jesus was addressing demons, He was not addressing fallen angels but unclean spirits. So it is essential to note that these were perverse or unclean spirits—the rebellious and disembodied spirits of the hybrid people who lived before the flood. That is why they seek embodiment because they once had a body.

In the Old Testament, we mostly read about wars in the flesh; there were many battles between the people of God and those giant hybrid races. Joshua, David, and others dealt with them through physical warfare. We do not see much demonic activity until David appears. When observing David's life, you can see a parallel between the natural and spiritual realms. At one point, satan rose up against David and tempted him to sin by counting his fighting men (1 Chronicles 21:1–8). The law forbid the kings to put confidence in their fighting armies. So when he ordered the armies to be counted, satan was actually fighting against Israel. We start to see in that passage that the unseen demonic realm influences the natural realm.

What did the Holy Spirit reveal to you regarding this chapter?

_____

_____

_____

_____

_____

_____

CHAPTER 2

THE ENEMY'S COVERT OPERATION

Put on the whole armor of God, that you may be able to stand against the wiles of the devil.

—Ephesians 6:11

In the previous chapter, we discussed how demons came to be. As mentioned, the demonic realm was not revealed in the Bible until the time of King David. When we study David's life, we will see how spiritual warfare directly influenced his natural battles. After Goliath was killed, his spirit was disembodied because that is what happened with the hybrid beings. Today, we are still warring with these disembodied spirits.

PARALLEL REALMS

David faced many struggles throughout his life and was essentially driven into sin. His trials were the workings of demonic spirits that fought against him. People in the Old Testament did not have the help we have today. They did not have the name of Jesus, spiritual gifts, or the Holy Spirit inside them.

And it shall come to pass in that day, that his burden shall be taken away from off thy shoulder, and his yoke from off thy neck, and the yoke shall be destroyed because of the anointing.

—Isaiah 10:27 KJV

In the Old Testament, God's people had prophets, priests, and kings, who had the Holy Spirit upon them but not within them. As New Testament believers, we now have the anointing both upon and within us (John 14:16–17). That which is within us is much more powerful than that which is upon us; however, when it comes to the anointing, it breaks the yoke, so we want as much as we can get.

In some Old Testament accounts, prophets reveal what happened behind the scenes in the unseen realm. For example, Ezekiel addresses both the natural and spiritual rulers of Tyre. In Ezekiel 28:1–10, he confronted a man; then you see a shift in verses 11–18 where he exposed the fallen covering cherub in the Garden of Eden—satan himself. Similarly, Isaiah prophesied against Babylon's prideful, earthly king in Isaiah 14:3–11. Then, in verses 12–17, he pronounced the judgment of helel, who lifted himself up against God in pride. Again, we see satan behind the scenes. These are just two examples of how the parallel realms operate together.

Even though we have a glimpse of spiritual warfare through the Old Testament prophets, Paul addressed this subject in more detail throughout the New Testament. He explains the armor that God has given us to stand against the demonic realm in Ephesians 6 and 2 Corinthians 10. Interestingly, he does not talk much about the entities themselves but focuses more on instructing believers to execute their authority and gain victory over them.

USING YOUR AUTHORITY

In conclusion, be strong in the Lord [draw your strength from Him and be empowered through the union with Him] and in the power of his [boundless] might. Put on the full armor of God [for his precepts are like the splendid armor of a heavily-armed soldier], so that you may be able to [successfully] stand up against all the schemes and the strategies and the deceits of the devil. For our struggle is not against flesh and blood [contending only with physical opponents], but against the rulers, against the powers, against the world forces of this [present] darkness, against the spiritual forces of wickedness in the heavenly (supernatural) places. Therefore, put on the complete armor of God, so that you will be able to [successfully] resist and stand your ground in the day of evil [of danger], and having done everything [that the crisis demands], to stand firm [in your place, fully prepared, immovable, victorious]. So stand firm and hold your ground, having tightened the wide band of truth (personal integrity, moral courage) around your waist and having put on the breastplate of righteousness (an upright heart), and having strapped on your feet the gospel of peace in preparation [to face the enemy with firm-footed stability and readiness produced by good news]. Above all, lift up the protective shield of faith with which you can extinguish all the flaming arrows of the evil one. And take the helmet of salvation, and the sword of the Spirit, which is the Word of God.

—Ephesians 6:10–17 AMP

Ephesians 6, the most descriptive chapter in the Bible for spiritual warfare, explains the armor of God. Notice how this chapter is worded; we are actually defending the faith. We are not obtaining anything because we already have all that we need.

Paul charged believers to take a stand in every situation as though they own and occupy territory in the Kingdom of God. With this armor, we are instructed to stand guard and defend what we have been given through Christ. Notice that most of the pieces of armor are defensive, not offensive. The only offensive weapon is the sword of the Spirit, God's Word. This sword should be used aggressively against the enemy. We must understand our armor.

Paul mentions four different sectors of opponents that are not flesh and blood that war against people; in other words, they are not human beings. Notice that in the Old Testament, everybody went to war against each other. As we discussed, there was no discernment about evil spirits until David came along. The first mention of an evil spirit in the Bible is the one that Saul dealt

Paul charged believers to take a stand in every situation as though they own and occupy territory in the Kingdom of God.

with, which is significant (1 Samuel 16:14–23). When that spirit would come and harass him, David played the harp, and it would leave.

There is no mention of demons before the one that distressed Saul. As previously mentioned, disembodied spirits were there from the hybrids who perished in the flood. In the Hebrew language, they are not labeled as angels. Different words are used for angels, which are not used in 1 Samuel 16. The Bible is distinct in the description of evil spirits versus angels.

The New Testament gives us more details about spiritual warfare. Amazingly, Paul said we are not wrestling against physical opponents, which is what they did in the Old Testament. They were constantly fighting because the hybrids were alive. Post-flood, God's people still warred with those half-breeds, which God wanted them to do; however, remember, by that time, behind the scenes, millions of disembodied, evil spirits were also among them. So it was quite a struggle.

DEMONIC DIVISIONS

Today, we are contending against rulers, powers, world forces of this present darkness, and spiritual forces of wickedness in the heavenly, supernatural places. So Ephesians 6:12 mentions four different divisions. Even though Paul does not go into much detail, they are all significant. Perhaps he personally expounded on the topic with congregations like the church in Ephesus; maybe he assumed they were already familiar with these divisions. I want to find more material on the people from that time. Would it not be nice to have the notes of those who attended Paul's meetings? All we know from Scripture is that there are these four divisions, which are all important.

Even after significant study, it is still unclear what these beings in Ephesians 6 really are. Yet I can tell you that I have encountered different species and levels in spiritual warfare. You have too. There has been quite a bit of confusion because it is not like what has been taught and depicted, such as the image of the red devil with horns and a pitchfork.

Only once have I seen a creature with horns: a very tall hideous giant being that stood upright and appeared to be half human and half goat. Somebody walked into our house in Seattle, so I went upstairs, and there it was, at least eight or nine feet tall. It would have had to stoop to get through the door if it even used doors. He was just standing there. When I researched it later, I found a picture of baal. That is who it was; I cannot even describe the hideousness.

If you do a study on baal, you can see that the image of this figure appears in many events today, such as commercials and satanic rituals on TV before ball games. You can look it up on the internet and see that same being. I do not recommend staring at these images, but we are seeing them more publicly. They even appear on T-shirts and in different stores. I believe that this baal creature that appeared in my house was lucifer.

> *They have also built the high places of baal, to burn their sons with fire for burnt offerings to baal, which I did not command or speak, nor did it come into My mind.*
>
> —Jeremiah 19:5 NIV

In the Old Testament, children were sacrificed to baal on altars. If you research what is happening in our culture and world, you can see that children are still being offered to baal in various ways. I now understand that baal is actually satan. He is just one being.

I have also seen other types of evil entities parading themselves in different ways. Some look like angels, whereas others look like creatures from another planet, but they are not. These are demons from a specific hierarchy.

Demonic entities come in many different forms, including those that look like lizards and furry animals. We mainly deal with the earthbound demons, which we were given authority over through Christ. Luke 10:19 says we have dominion over serpents and scorpions, which are symbolic of demons who walk or crawl along the ground. So we have been given authority over earthbound demons, which does not go over well with many people, but that is just how it is. Jesus essentially came as a human being and dealt with those entities that human beings now have authority over, which are disembodied spirits.

> *For the idols speak delusion; The diviners envision lies, and tell false dreams; They comfort in vain. Therefore the people wend their way like sheep; They are in trouble because there is no shepherd.*
>
> —Zechariah 10:2

The Bible mentions different heavenly beings, such as seraphim and cherubim (Isaiah 6:1–3; Ezekiel 10:14). We have already discussed the Nephilim, which are fallen angels who are now chained. There are also teraphim.[3] This word is derived from terra, which means "earthbound." In several Scriptures, teraphim are mentioned as idols, such as the household gods that Jacob's wife, Rachel, stole from her father, Laban (Genesis 31:19).

However, if we dive a little deeper, the Bible reveals that they are those disembodied, earthbound demons that masquerade themselves. For example, Zechariah 10:2 describes the idols as speaking delusion. It was not the wood and stone talking but the disembodied spirits hiding behind them. They used deception to gain access and occupy people, aiming to infiltrate genetics.

INFILTRATION OF HUMAN DNA

If you research, you find that the enemy is still seeking to alter human DNA, just like in the days of Noah—it is happening again. One way to get into the DNA and change people's genetics is through the liver. This corruption has occurred through disease-causing bacteria that mutate in the human body. Classified information shows that certain strains of bacteria are living organisms that can change the human liver. So these entities use this to work their way into your DNA.

If you want to know how the serpent infiltrated the blood of a human being, you can research mutations that came from bacteria affecting the liver. However,

---

3. "H8655 - tᵊrāp̄îm - Strong's Hebrew Lexicon," Blue Letter Bible, accessed July 9, 2023, https://www.blueletterbible.org/lexicon/h8655/kjv/wlc/0-1/.

you must be careful when doing this type of research because you will be tracked. You can observe that the Bible gives many clues about the covert strategies of the enemy that are hidden behind the scenes. If you study the liver and the impact of these bacteria on human beings, you will see how this infiltration occurs. DNA–altering bacteria are not of God; they are microscopic demonic entities. God did not create bacteria to be rogue and harmful, yet they can be carriers that can penetrate and change the human DNA. These truths are hidden from the masses.

To summarize, the hierarchy of demonic forces, mentioned in Ephesians 6, aims to infiltrate and influence the human race. As such, satan wants to accelerate this so that he can obtain the human race as fast as possible. The enemy would have prevailed if God had not slowed everything down. He destroyed the earth once, kept eight pure people, and restarted the world. Even afterward, these genetically altered hybrids appeared again. God then raised up David, Samson, and others to kill off all these giant races.

In the Old Testament, God's people were forbidden to interbreed with certain races because they had hybrid DNA. The Israelites were separated as a people because God wanted a human race of pure stock so that when Jesus came in the flesh, He would come as a pure human being. Then, He would be the perfect sacrifice. If He had any altered DNA in His blood that was hybrid or from the serpent's seed, He would not have been able to redeem us. So although satan tried to prevent it from happening, God preserved the human race. Jesus came through Mary, a pure human being. All the genealogies show that her lines did not interbreed with these races of people on the earth at different times. So Jesus became a pure and spotless lamb without blemish, genetic defect, or any reptilian blood in Him.

We are called to resist and obtain dominion over earthbound entities through the truth that Jesus already defeated them.

STAY WITHIN GOD'S BOUNDARIES

In spiritual warfare, we are dealing with the four levels of entities that Paul mentioned. We are called to resist and obtain dominion over them through the truth that Jesus already defeated them. However, it does not say that individually, we have power over all the enemy, but Luke 10:19 states that we are to trample on serpents and scorpions, which are the earthbound ones that crawl along the ground. It does not mention trampling on other entities, so we must stay within our parameters.

Some individuals presumptuously confronted entities by themselves, but God never gave them authority to deal with those entities. These people were killed. Intercessors have prayed against demonic powers in the heavenly realms, which unfortunately cost them their lives. Previously, I did not understand why I was losing so many good people in my life. They were bold and came against these entities in high places outside the Holy Spirit's leading.

Clearly, Jesus only dealt with the unclean spirits and earthbound demons from the hybrid races. When Jesus was on earth, He drove demons out of people; He did not directly expel principalities or powers from their position in the atmosphere. He said He saw satan fall like lightning, but He does not even mention any of these other levels that Paul does. We do not know much about these different entities; therefore, it's wise for us to stay within the boundaries of authority that the Lord has given us through His Word.

What did the Holy Spirit reveal to you regarding this chapter?

CHAPTER 3

PARAMETERS OF SPIRITUAL AUTHORITY

So Jesus said, "I speak to you eternal truth.
The Son is unable to do anything from Himself
or through His own initiative. I only do the
works that I see the Father doing, for the
Son does the same works as His Father."

—John 5:19 TPT

The groundwork for deliverance has been established in the first two chapters. We discussed how Jesus only dealt with demons inhabiting people; He did not address those that were not in people. By now, we understand that entities are everywhere that do not dwell in people. Paul lists this hierarchy in Ephesians 6. However, Jesus did not directly deal with those. He delivered people from earthbound, disembodied spirits, the same demons that we are charged to trample. Although Jesus defeated all the enemy's army on the cross, the ultimate enforcement of this victory over these other entities will take place at the end of the age when they are all thrown into the lake of fire (Revelation 20:7–10).

TERRITORIAL SPIRITS IN THE AIR

These [kings] have one purpose [one mind, one common goal], and they give their power and authority to the beast. They will wage war against the Lamb (Christ), and the Lamb will triumph and conquer them, because He is Lord of lords and King of kings, and those who are with Him and on His side are the called and chosen (elect) and faithful.

—Revelation 17:13–14 AMP

In the future, Jesus, the saints, and angels will come, wage war, and conquer the enemy's army. As mentioned, I have lost some friends who presumptuously engaged these entities in spiritual warfare.

Over the following several years, I investigated this and uncovered more information. When my research was complete, I had exhausted mysterious subjects, including UFOs and dinosaurs. My initial research process generated more questions; toward the end, especially concerning UFOs, I came to unquestionable conclusions. I finally just took all my work and destroyed it.

Through my research, I realized that those levels of entities we are dealing with have to do with the coming end-time deception. Too much detail about these subjects will cause division and confusion because people are not ready; I was not even prepared for what I found out. Maybe you are, but I must be wise concerning the information I release because I learned that world governments are involved. Therefore, there is no reason to address something the Bible does not discuss.

Since demonic influence has infiltrated governments, when you start to understand and communicate what is happening with these entities we have been discussing, you will also find yourself dealing with authorities in the flesh. The Lord has not called me to do that. Maybe He has called someone else to that assignment. I am called to preach the gospel and minister deliverance as part of the package.

> *In the same way, these people—who claim authority from their dreams—live immoral lives, defy authority, and scoff at supernatural beings. But even Michael, one of the mightiest of the angels, did not dare accuse the devil of blasphemy, but simply said, "The Lord rebuke you!"* (This took place when Michael was arguing with the devil about Moses' body.)
>
> —Jude 1:8–9 NLT

We must stay within God's set boundaries when dealing with spiritual warfare; do not be presumptuous. Each one of us needs help in fighting these evil spirits. The various entities in the higher places are not part of the earthbound demons we have been given the authority to deal with directly.

The corporate anointing upon a congregation of believers can come against these spirits when the Lord permits them. When the body of Christ comes together, there is greater power in agreement because of the numbers. So at times, we can confront these spirits as a body. Still, individually, we have been given authority over serpents, scorpions, and all the enemy's power— the evil spirits on the earth.

The book of Revelation speaks of demonic rulers influencing our world leaders—those who are at a high level and can control countries (Revelation 17). The church of the Lord Jesus Christ could agree and push back these entities; however, it is not wise for individuals to attempt this.

> For Jesus had already said to the spirit, "Come out of the man, you evil spirit." Then Jesus demanded, "What is your name?" And he replied, "My name is Legion, because there are many of us inside this man." Then the evil spirits begged him again and again not to send them to some distant place.
>
> There happened to be a large herd of pigs feeding on the hillside nearby. "Send us into those pigs," the spirits begged. "Let us enter them." So Jesus gave them permission. The evil spirits came out of the man and entered the pigs, and the

entire herd of about 2,000 pigs plunged down the steep hillside into the lake and drowned in the water.

So the man started off to visit the Ten Towns of that region and began to proclaim the great things Jesus had done for him; and everyone was amazed at what he told them.

—Mark 5:8–13, 20 NLT

People may encounter higher-level entities that do not necessarily inhabit people but control the lower-level disembodied spirits in a particular area who do. There are territorial strongholds in cities and regions, so you may sometimes bump into more than just the spirits you drive out of people. Jesus faced this situation when He was driving out demons and encountered legion (Mark 5:1–20; Luke 8:26–39). I believe that legion was the entity that was a stronghold over that city and territory. You may encounter something similar.

Ruling spirits, the powers dominating the nations, have performed feats that people cannot do today. The pyramids and mysterious marks on the earth were accomplished with help from entities in high places. From the air, you can see tattoos on the planet. There were no airplanes at the time when they were created, yet people somehow had the ability to be in the air.

Why would someone create designs that point directly toward true or magnetic north when viewed from the air? These would not be needed unless you were in the air. These actions were hidden from us. I believe that governments have hidden these findings from the public because satan, the prince of the power of the air, wants to keep his tactics covert.

BE PREPARED
FOR RESISTANCE

Therefore submit to God. Resist the devil and he will flee from you.

—James 4:7

But thanks be to God, who gives us the victory through our Lord Jesus Christ. Therefore, my beloved brethren, be steadfast, immovable, always abounding in the work of the Lord, knowing that your labor is not in vain in the Lord.

—1 Corinthians 15:57–58

We are given authority to deal with earthbound demons in people and are instructed to resist them, standing our ground in the evil day. According to 1 Corinthians 15:57–58, we must remain immovable, stay in our place, and be victorious, tightening everything up and holding our ground. Ephesians 6 gives us all the different pieces of protective armor. It does not tell us to be aggressive but to stand firm.

When evening came, they brought to Him many who were under the power of demons; and He cast out the evil spirits with a word, and restored to health all who were sick [exhibiting His authority as Messiah].

—Matthew 8:16 AMP

It is worth mentioning again that I do not go searching for these territorial spirits. Jesus did not go out and look for demons; they came at Him when He arrived in different places (Mark 5:2). He was not looking for them and did not call them out. This is a paradigm shift for many people, but Scripture clearly says this. I am not looking for a battle or spiritual warfare. I am not seeking it; however, it will come because I am sent.

If you are sent somewhere on an assignment, the idea in Ephesians 6 is that you are dressed for it. You are prepared to defend what God has sent you to do. You are on a mission and will accomplish it, yet you will face resistance during that mission. That is the whole concept of spiritual warfare; it is what Jesus did throughout His earthly ministry. He did not uproot the devil or

I am not looking for a battle or spiritual warfare. I am not seeking it; however, it will come because I am sent.

pull-down strongholds from the air. He cast ground-level demons out of people and never even addressed the higher-ups.

FOCUS ON GOD'S ASSIGNMENT

When Jesus spoke with governmental authorities, such as Pilate and Herod, He never addressed the entities behind them (Luke 23:6–25). But wherever Jesus went, if a demon needed to be dealt with at the time, it manifested, and He drove it out. So think about the fact that Jesus never addressed territorial spirits that influenced world leaders. He was just out and about in the countryside or the synagogue, and these demon spirits would start manifesting. Jesus just preached the gospel; this is what we are supposed to do. I want to straighten this out and simplify it for you because it can be easy.

I do not go out looking for aliens, Big Foot, or different hierarchies of evil spirits. Jesus defeated every wicked entity on the cross, but He told us to cast out demons, which are essentially in people. So let us be honest: How many people have the spiritual sensitivity to know that a demon is in someone even if it doesn't talk or manifest? The bottom line is that most of the time, we know because they start to get fidgety. They begin speaking through the person and manifesting. This is what happened with Jesus.

Jesus was not looking for a fight. He was sent places to preach the gospel, and the demons got in the way, so they were driven out. In Ephesians 6, you find the first stage of the hierarchy, which can be dealt with on an individual level. The other three groups should be dealt with through the corporate body. Congregations of believers can displace territorial entities in their area when a strong presence of God is dwelling in their midst. You really have to be Spirit-led to take out these higher echelons, and it has to be done through the body of Christ.

To summarize what has been laid out, it is always best to stay within your parameters and understand that you are wearing protective armor. The sword of the Spirit is the only offensive weapon; the rest of your armor is defensive. You are called to stand and defend the faith. In doing so, demons will find you; you do not need to seek them out. In fact, you should expect demons to find you. It is how Jesus dealt with the enemy, so that is how you should deal with them.

ALWAYS PRAY IN THE SPIRIT

With all prayer and petition pray [with specific requests] at all times [on every occasion and in every season] in the Spirit, and with this in view, stay alert with all perseverance and petition [interceding in prayer] for all God's people. And pray for me, that words may be given to me when I open my mouth, to proclaim boldly the mystery of the good news [of salvation], for

which I am an ambassador in chains. And pray
that in proclaiming it I may speak boldly and
courageously, as I should.

—Ephesians 6:18–20 AMP

> **True warfare is being completely dressed in the defensive armor and praying in the Spirit at all times with all types of prayer in every season.**

After listing all the armor in Ephesians 6, verse 18 instructs us to pray in the Spirit all the time, everywhere we go. With this in mind, we must stay alert and persevere in intercession for God's people. Then Paul asks for prayer for the words and boldness to proclaim the gospel. He explains that he is an ambassador in chains. Guess who put him in chains? It was the devil. In his letter, Paul gave the Ephesians all the information he could share about spiritual warfare, and then he essentially said, "Now pray."

True warfare is being completely dressed in the defensive armor and praying in the Spirit at all times with all types of prayer in every season. We must maintain this stance, stay alert, and persevere in prayer for all God's people.

Paul asked the Ephesians to pray for him. His thought process behind this request is that because he was in chains, he wanted boldness to open his mouth and proclaim the mystery of the good news of salvation. He described himself as an "ambassador in chains." He was in jail, which was a result of spiritual warfare. As Paul said, we are supposed to be praying.

> As the [ten] toes of the feet were partly of iron and partly of clay, so some of the kingdom will be strong, and another part of it will be brittle. And as you saw the iron mixed with common clay, so they will combine with one another in the seed of men; but they will not merge [for such diverse things or ideologies cannot unite], even as iron does not mix with clay.
>
> —Daniel 2:42–43 AMP

These entities claim to be from another planet but are really from another realm. As the body of Christ prays, they will be exposed. They are part of the evil echelons of satan. Ultimately, they will try to intertwine themselves with the human race. Daniel 2 alludes to this in describing the image of the statue with different substances from the head down to the ten toes. Those of the kingdom mentioned in verses 42–43 tried to mix with the seed of men, but it would not take, just like clay cannot mix with iron. You may be thinking, It's unclear who "they" refers to in this passage, but I'm telling you who they are.

For the coming of the Son of Man (the Messiah)
will be just like the days of Noah.

—Matthew 24:37 AMP

Daniel saw that some kind of mixture would happen within the human race at the end of days, symbolized by the ten toes of iron and clay. Daniel 2:43 says, "They will combine with one another in the seed of men, but they will not merge." Jesus warned us that before His coming at the end, it would be like it was in the days of Noah (Matthew 24:37–39).

As I mentioned, there are ways to alter human DNA today, the same way people were hybridized in Noah's day. There is a way to do it through the liver via bacteria; certain diseases and viruses are created as messengers that alter genetics. You must be very careful. The bottom line is that your immune system needs to be boosted to keep yourself pure so that these DNA-altering substances do not infiltrate you.

All kinds of chemicals and substances are processed in our foods. Multiple environmental factors are coming against our immune system. Our adversary, satan, wants to break down our natural defenses so that even common viruses that we would typically be able to fight off could enter our genetics through our weakened immune system. Spiritually, you must be aware of this; physically, you need to keep your immune system strong.

REVELATION COMES
WITH MATURITY

Essentially, all believers are given the authority to drive out demons that Jesus defeated. We, the body of Christ, are called to resist the enemy and take our stand so that the gospel can be proclaimed, just like Paul said. This is the background of spiritual warfare.

> *And the disciples came and said to Him, "Why do You speak to them in parables?" He answered and said to them, "Because it has been given to you to know the mysteries of the kingdom of heaven, but to them it has not been given."*
>
> —Matthew 13:10–11

Not much is written about spiritual warfare in the New Testament, but there is a reason for the apparent information deficit. I believe it is hidden because Jesus spoke to the masses in parables. As I have, you need to dig for revelation by studying the Scriptures. I discovered hidden truths in God's Word that revealed some nuggets that were not apparent on the surface.

Jesus explained the mysteries of the parables to the disciples so they would eventually be able to share them with the world once they understood. One moment, they did not get the message of the parables; then after Jesus spoke with them, their eyes were opened. He said it was given to them—but not to the masses—to know the mysteries. He probably did it that way because certain people are not mature enough and would not use this information correctly. It would not be advantageous for them or God. Some people are just not ready. We must accept that God has not given certain mysteries to everyone.

If you seek God and show maturity, He will reveal what you are ready for. That is why I am cautious; I do not feel I am supposed to share everything God has revealed. If you ask God, He will show you the answers in time. I have been studying some subjects for twenty to twenty-five years. I researched a certain topic for three years; once I found out the truth, I destroyed everything. I had all the evidence you would need to win a case, including photos and letters. Then I realized this information is being hidden because people are not ready for it. The coming deception has to do with the end-time scenario; however, it does not involve the body of Christ. God's remnant will not be deceived; they will be in the know.

What did the Holy Spirit reveal to you regarding this chapter?

_____

_____

_____

_____

_____

CHAPTER 4

THE BATTLE FOR YOUR MIND

*And do not be conformed to this world, but
be transformed by the renewing of your
mind, that you may prove what is that good
and acceptable and perfect will of God.*

—Romans 12:2

We have explored some great Scriptures in the previous chapters, revealing what has been happening behind the scenes throughout history. Before diving into the process of deliverance, we will uncover the enemy's mode of operation. It is essential to understand his strategies.

We do not always need to know which specific entity type we are dealing with. Just know, as it has been emphasized, that we should not endeavor to confront certain spirits, such as territorial spirits over our cities or states unless we do this in a corporate setting. In Ephesians 6, after Paul described the different spiritual echelons and our protective armor, he concluded that we are to stand firm and pray on all occasions with all kinds of prayer.

For the Son of Man has come to seek and to save that which was lost.

—Luke 19:10

Remember, Jesus did not pick a fight with the devil. Demons manifested as He was doing God's will. Despite what deliverance ministries have taught, we should not chase demons. During His earthly ministry, Jesus was seeking those who were lost. He wanted people to be saved, healed, and delivered; however, He was not doing spiritual warfare by picking a fight. Jesus did the will of the Father, and along the way, He encountered demonic resistance.

WAGING WAR IN THE SPIRIT

For though we walk in the flesh [as mortal men], we are not carrying on our [spiritual] warfare according to the flesh and using the weapons of man. The weapons of our warfare are not physical [weapons of flesh and blood]. Our weapons are divinely powerful for the destruction of fortresses. We are destroying sophisticated arguments and every exalted and proud thing that sets itself up against the [true] knowledge of God, and we are taking every thought and purpose captive to the obedience of Christ, being ready to punish every act of disobedience, when your own obedience [as a church] is complete.

—2 Corinthians 10:3–6 AMP

Second Corinthians 10 sounds similar to what Paul said in Ephesians 6. He explains that we are not using physical weapons of flesh and blood and reveals our spiritual warfare—destroying any argument that sets itself up above the knowledge of God. We wage war by taking every thought captive, which originates from the soul realm, and subjecting them to the obedience of Christ. This passage builds upon everything we have been discussing in the previous chapters.

Paul specifically wrote this way for a reason. I encourage you to study his epistles to understand the essence of what he was communicating. He had an indescribable encounter with God when he was caught up in paradise, and thankfully, you can glean from what he was permitted to share. But he was not allowed to share many things (2 Corinthians 12:4). Likewise, the Lord showed me revelations

> **We wage war by taking every thought captive, which originates from the soul realm, and subjecting them to the obedience of Christ.**

that I am forbidden to share, some of which have to do with spiritual warfare; however, I will reveal what the Lord permits.

Spiritual weapons have been given to us, which can be used to dismantle fortresses or strongholds. Scripture instructs us to tear down every proud argument that sets itself up above the knowledge of God, which is the revelation that has already been given to us through the gospel. We must take every thought captive and make them obedient to Christ—that is our warfare and our responsibility. God will not take our thoughts captive; we need to do that. The disobedience of wicked spirits is punished when our obedience as a church is complete.

> *Now the Spirit expressly says that in latter times some will depart from the faith, giving heed to deceiving spirits and doctrines of demons, speaking lies in hypocrisy, having their own conscience seared with a hot iron.*
>
> —1 Timothy 4:1–2

The Bible reveals that the higher-level echelons of demons will not reap destruction until the end. But we are now instructed to bring correction. Throughout the New Testament, Paul constantly corrected false doctrine and wrong perceptions. Through his teaching, he brought people back into God's way. He warned Timothy that there would be all kinds of false doctrine in the last days. People will be self-seeking and lovers of themselves; some will be so wicked and evil that they will even sell out their parents (2 Timothy 3:1–5). We already see this taking place. Paul's letters have been preparing the body of Christ for our last days, which are perilous times full of all wickedness.

THOUGHTS ARE A GATEWAY

Now the serpent was more cunning than any beast of the field which the Lord God had made. And he said to the woman, "Has God indeed said, 'You shall not eat of every tree of the garden'?"

—Genesis 3:1

The demonic realm gains entry into the human race through the thought process. Before the fall, Adam and Eve were impenetrable. The enemy could only gain access by deceiving them, causing them to accept a lie. That was difficult to do, mainly because they were hedged in, just like Job, and satan could not get to them. He had to be cunning and crafty to infiltrate their minds.

How you are fallen from heaven, O lucifer, son of the morning! How you are cut down to the ground, You who weakened the nations! For you have said in your heart: "I will ascend into heaven, I will exalt my throne above the stars

of God; I will also sit on the mount of the con-
gregation on the farthest sides of the north; I
will ascend above the heights of the clouds, I
will be like the Most High."

—Isaiah 14:12–14

How did the devious serpent end up with Adam and Eve in the Garden of Eden? In Genesis 3:1, the Hebrew word for serpent is nahash,[4] which also can mean "enlightened one."[5] This word seems uncannily similar to helel,[6] the Hebrew word translated to English as lucifer in Isaiah 14:12, which means "bright and shiny one." I am not sure why the translators used the wording they decided on; however, the point is that it looks like both words, nahash and helel, describe the same being.

You were in Eden, the garden of God; Every
precious stone was your covering: The sardius,
topaz, and diamond, beryl, onyx, and jasper,
sapphire, turquoise, and emerald with gold.
The workmanship of your timbrels and pipes
was prepared for you on the day you were
created. You were the anointed cherub who
covers; I established you; You were on the holy

4. "H5175 - *nāḥāš* - Strong's Hebrew Lexicon," *Blue Letter Bible,* accessed July 12, 2023. https://www.blueletterbible.org/lexicon/h5175/kjv/wlc/0-1/.

5. "Etymology of the Name Nahash," Abiram Publications, April 19, 2006, https://www.abarim-publications.com/Meaning/Nahash.html.

6. "Helel," *Blue Letter Bible.*

mountain of God; You walked back and forth in the midst of the fiery stones. You were perfect in your ways from the day you were created, till iniquity was found in you.

—Ezekiel 28:13–16

Ezekiel 28:13–16 describes the same entity in Genesis 3 and Isaiah 14: satan. God initially assigned him to the garden as an anointed covering cherub; however, he became lifted up in pride because of his beauty and started considering himself as important. Satan may have even partaken of the forbidden fruit in the Garden of Eden. He fell first—then, he got Adam and Eve to fall so he could infiltrate the human race and attack God out of jealousy. This fallen cherub started all the competition that takes place among humanity today. Just as he did with Adam and Eve, he still uses the same strategy of deceptive thoughts to infiltrate people's lives.

Before Noah's flood, satan's crafty efforts of infiltrating the human race seemed to succeed for a moment. As we discussed, he thought he could stop the Messiah from coming in a human body because he had corrupted the genetics. We discussed the material that altered the DNA; a reptilian type of blood, the serpent's seed, could get into human beings through disease or viruses processed in the liver. God intervened by destroying the world and starting fresh with the eight people He preserved. The disembodied hybrid spirits are now wandering the earth, still seeking to infiltrate the human race.

HIJACKED THROUGH DECEPTION

It is noteworthy to remember that the Nephilim taught the people to interbreed, so they had to believe a lie and give access to the seed of the serpent. Similar corruption will happen again at the end of days—it has already started. The gateway for this demonic infiltration and corruption of human genetics is through deception, just like in Genesis. Many people will believe the enemy's lies and allow their bodies to be genetically compromised, which is why I emphasize the importance of being spiritually aware and taking action to build up your immune system.

Demons or disembodied spirits are territorial because they remain in the same area they were in before the flood. When the flood came, the hybrid people drowned and lost their bodies; however, their spirits are still on earth in a parallel realm. It does not matter whether a spirit is underwater or on the land because they are in a different dimension. They are not restricted like we are. They have other parameters in the spirit realm.

Since spirit beings of all levels are shut out of this physical realm, the only way they can have any kind of expression is to hijack human beings. By getting humans to interbreed, these entities can enter the physical realm, which is why God stopped their interbreeding with the flood. After the flood, David had to take out the giant races because human blood was compromised again.

The Bible doesn't give us much information about demons until Jesus came. When He arrived, the demonic spirits knew who He was. They also knew what Jesus could and could not do as the Son of Man. The unclean spirits did not want to move out of their area or be sent into the torment of hell before their time (Matthew 8:29). There was a specific timeline, so Jesus did not send them to the pit during His earthly ministry; if He had, the Bible would have said so.

> *I tell you this timeless truth: The person who follows Me in faith, believing in Me, will do the same mighty miracles that I do—even greater miracles than these because I go to be with My Father!*
>
> —John 14:12 TPT

Jesus is the Son of God, but He came to the world as the Son of Man, operating in a man's body by the anointing of the Holy Spirit; therefore, He could tell the disciples that they could do the same works. After the disciples, Jesus sent out seventy-two others (Luke 10:1), and then He said that everyone who believes in Him would operate in the same power of the Holy Spirit. He declared in John 14:12 that a day would come when we would do even greater works than He did.

Jesus did everything as the Son of Man. Even though He was the Son of God, He laid that aside and became a servant (Philippians 2:5–11) who did everything under the anointing of the Holy Spirit. He went through life as we all do and was baptized to fulfill all righteousness (Matthew 3:13–15). Jesus understood what it was like to be tempted by the devil (Matthew 4:1–11). He had to cast down the enemy's lies by using God's Word to resist satan in the wilderness, just like we do. He essentially fulfilled everything people would need and became the ultimate sacrifice. Through His life, Jesus taught us how to navigate spiritual warfare.

THE MANIFOLD WISDOM OF GOD

When Jesus went forth in the power of the Spirit, the demons recognized who He was, and they started to manifest. Until that point, for the most part, when people in the Bible would speak or act, we do not read about many demonic manifestations. Before Jesus, the influence of the spirit realm remained mainly behind the scenes.

> And as you go, preach, saying, "The kingdom of heaven is at hand." Heal the sick, cleanse the lepers, raise the dead, cast out demons. Freely you have received, freely give.
>
> —Matthew 10:7–8

We have been given the name and the blood of Jesus; the finished work of the cross is now in effect (John 19:30). Today, we are commissioned to go forth and drive out devils, period. We are not supposed to argue with them, converse with them, investigate, or look for them; we are instructed to drive them out.

Believers are sent to preach the gospel. But in response to that gospel message, the dead will be raised; the sick will be healed; there will be Jubilee—debt forgiveness—and sins will be forgiven. We will also see devils driven out of people. That is our assignment as the body of Christ.

> *And to make all see what is the fellowship of the mystery, which from the beginning of the ages has been hidden in God who created all things through Jesus Christ; to the intent that now the manifold wisdom of God might be made known by the church to the principalities and powers in the heavenly places, according to the eternal purpose which He accomplished in Christ Jesus our Lord.*
>
> —Ephesians 3:9–11

Jesus's crucifixion and resurrection destroyed the works of the devil behind the scenes. However, entities are still in place, ruling and reigning through world leaders. They appear to be unaffected by what has happened on the cross. That is why I explained to you that their defeat will not be evident until we enforce the victory through the revelation of the manifold wisdom of God, expressed in Ephesians 3:9–11. The mystery is that as this wisdom is revealed through the church, it brings judgment to the powers of the air. Through the body of Christ, God will reveal Himself to the principalities, which will execute this judgment; this will not happen through an individual.

CORRECT VIEW OF SPIRITUAL WARFARE

From that time Jesus began to show His disciples that He must go to Jerusalem, and suffer many things from the elders and chief priests and scribes, and be killed, and be raised the third day. Then Peter took Him aside and began to rebuke Him, saying, "Far be it from You, Lord; this shall not happen to You!" But He turned and said to Peter, "Get behind Me, Satan! You are an offense to Me, for you are not mindful of the things of God, but of the things of men."

—Matthew 16:20–23

In 2 Corinthians 10:5, we are admonished to cast down arguments and every false idea that comes against the knowledge of God. The dialog between Jesus and Peter in Matthew 16:21–23 is a perfect example. After

Jesus expressed that He would be turned over to the authorities and crucified, Peter rebuked Him and said it would not happen. Jesus then addressed him as satan and told him his ideas were not from God. This is the proper way to look at spiritual warfare.

Today, we have an overabundance of deliverance teaching and ministries; however, the gospel did not focus on that. Deliverance was never meant to be compartmentalized. When advancing the gospel, it is among other demonstrations, such as healing the sick and raising the dead. One is not more challenging to perform than the other.

When you encounter demons, you drive them out; you are not supposed to look for them or label your meetings. As such, you should see other manifestations of God's power in addition to deliverance. Even though deliverance is part of the gospel, Jesus did not focus only on that; He preached and demonstrated the whole gospel message.

Everything I have shared with you is to establish a firm foundation based on the Word of God. It is not a complete study of the origins of spiritual warfare, which would take months. If you want more information, you can get my three-volume Holy Fire set, which will explain many of these topics in greater detail. This series totals about nine hundred pages and discusses the origin and operation of the demonic and reveals how satan does not want you to walk in holiness and the holy fire.

> **Jesus did not focus only on deliverance; He preached and demonstrated the whole gospel message.**

As the church, we must be ready to punish all disobedience by fulfilling our obedience as the body, according to 2 Corinthians 10:6. You must look at what the Word of God precisely says and not make it something it is not. I have made it very simple for you because it is not complicated at all. In the chapters ahead, I will show you how to fortify your walk with God so that you can see deliverance.

What did the Holy Spirit reveal to you regarding this chapter?

_____

_____

_____

_____

_____

_____

_____

_____

_____

_____

_____

_____

_____

_____

_____

_____

_____

_____

_____

_____

_____

_____

CHAPTER 5

THE TRUTH SETS CAPTIVES FREE

*The Spirit of the Lord is upon Me, because
He has anointed Me to preach the gospel
to the poor; He has sent Me to heal the
brokenhearted, to proclaim liberty to the
captives and recovery of sight to the blind,
to set at liberty those who are oppressed; To
proclaim the acceptable year of the Lord.*

—Luke 4:18–19

The basis of the gospel message is found in Luke 4:18–19. Jesus is actually reading a prophecy about Himself from Isaiah (Isaiah 61:1–3) that tells us the Holy Spirit anointed Him to preach the gospel specifically to the poor. Jesus was sent to heal the brokenhearted, recover sight for the blind, and preach deliverance to the captives. If you are captive, then you need deliverance. Setting at liberty those who are oppressed means breaking shackles. Preaching the favorable year of the Lord refers to the fulfillment of Jubilee, which is debt forgiveness (Leviticus 25:10). This is the foundation of the gospel message.

DELIVERANCE IS NOT EXCLUSIVE

And He said to them, "As you go into all the world, preach openly the wonderful news of the gospel to the entire human race! Whoever believes the good news and is baptized will be saved, and whoever does not believe the good news will be condemned. And these miracle signs will accompany those who believe: They will drive out demons in the power of My name. They will speak in tongues. They will be supernaturally protected from snakes and from drinking anything poisonous. And they will lay hands on the sick and heal them."

—Mark 16:15–18 TPT

The Spirit of the Lord was on Jesus to preach the gospel message and break the yokes of sickness and oppression off people. He allowed the Holy Spirit to manifest through His life to do the works written in Luke 4:18–19. Ministry was meant to be doing these works. All of us are qualified to preach the good news. Mark 16:17 expresses that miraculous signs will follow those who believe or the believing ones. This verse refers to all of us, not just fivefold ministers. I do not know how certain aspects of ministry became exclusive to the fivefold ministers because the gifts of the Spirit are for everybody. The Bible does not designate only certain people to operate in these gifts.

To understand the fivefold, let us take a moment to look at the apostle Paul's life. He was chosen to be an apostle since birth, yet he spent much of his life working against God and killing Christians (Galatians 1:13–16). He did not seem to have a choice because it was written that he would be an apostle. So for half of his life, he resisted God, and then he was arrested by the Lord on the road to Damascus. During this encounter, Paul recognized the Person in glistening clothes who spoke to him as Lord (Acts 9:1–6).

> *Now these are the gifts Christ gave to the church: the apostles, the prophets, the evangelists, and the pastors and teachers. Their responsibility is to equip God's people to do His work and build up the church, the body of Christ. This will continue until we all come to such unity in our faith and knowledge of God's Son that we will be mature in the Lord, measuring up to the full and complete standard of Christ.*
>
> —Ephesians 4:11–13 NLT

In every generation, God chooses fivefold ministers. He sets them in the church like a jeweler places gems within a setting. The idea is that they are part of God's plan and sent by Him; they do not appoint themselves. You can see that Paul did not have a choice. Jesus told him it was hard for him to kick against the goads (Acts 9:5). Goads were prods that would poke animals, such as cows, to move in a specific direction, gather together, or stay within their set boundaries. Jesus addressed Paul this way because He wanted to guide him onto the right path.

> *You did not choose Me, but I chose you and appointed you that you should go and bear fruit, and that your fruit should remain, that whatever you ask the Father in My name He may give you.*
>
> —John 15:16

Paul called Jesus "Lord" and experienced conversion; then afterward, he started to fulfill his apostleship. He said in his writings that he was appointed as an apostle since birth, much earlier than the road to Damascus. Jesus essentially said, "I chose you. You did not choose me." This means fivefold ministers are part of the church's foundation, which Christ sets and ordains; this differs from the gifts the Holy Spirit gives people as He wills.

> *But the manifestation of the Spirit is given to each one for the profit of all: for to one is given the word of wisdom through the Spirit, to another the word of knowledge through the same Spirit, to another faith by the same Spirit, to another gifts of healings by the same Spirit, to another the working of miracles, to another prophecy, to another discerning of spirits, to another different kinds of tongues, to another*

the interpretation of tongues. But one and the
same Spirit works all these things, distributing
to each one individually as He wills.

—1 Corinthians 12:7–11

The Holy Spirit gives out the gifts; each of us receives gifts according to the Spirit's discernment and will. Everyone has at least one of the gifts of the Spirit, which means that we all can and should operate in the supernatural. It is the same with driving out demons—all of us can do it. It is not just for the fivefold ministers; the gospel message is to be preached by all believing ones.

Notice there is no gift of casting out demons in 1 Corinthians 12:7–11 or anywhere else in the Bible. As believers, Jesus gave us all His name to drive out demons (Mark 16:17). This is not complicated, but because this aspect of ministry has not been taught correctly, many people misunderstand it; therefore, it does not work for them.

So then faith comes by hearing, and hearing by
the Word of God.

—Romans 10:17

We are all supposed to see healings, deliverances, and people raised from the dead, but if you do not emphasize this through teaching the Scripture and meditating on the truth, you will not see results. However, you will see the manifestation if you concentrate on certain truths.

On the other hand, many isolate specific subjects and may see results, but they leave out the rest of the gospel. The gospel message includes a variety of demonstrations. For example, in a crowd, some need deliverance, others need healing, some need debt cancellation, and someone may need to be raised from the dead. Some need good news because they are poor.

A GREATER COVENANT

Why was the gospel such good news when Israel was supposed to be a nation that God blessed? According to Deuteronomy 28:1–14, obedient people of God would be the head, not the tail; they would not have to borrow from anybody but would lend to people because they would own everything. The Scripture said that people from other nations would come and bow down to them. Their enemies would try to attack them from one way and end up fleeing in seven directions. The problem was that the people of Israel strayed away from God; however, in the New Testament, Jesus fulfilled all those promises of the old covenant.

> *Because finding fault with them, He says: "Behold, the days are coming, says the Lord, when I will make a new covenant with the house of Israel and with the house of Judah— not according to the covenant that I made with their fathers in the day when I took them by the hand to lead them out of the land of Egypt;*

*because they did not continue in My covenant,
and I disregarded them, says the Lord. For this
is the covenant that I will make with the house
of Israel after those days, says the Lord: I will
put My laws in their mind and write them on
their hearts; and I will be their God, and they
shall be My people."*

—Hebrews 8:8–10

The new covenant is a greater, better covenant with better promises based on the blood of Jesus. The new covenant includes the manifestations of the gospel that we have been discussing; one of them is deliverance.

In a previous chapter, we explored 2 Corinthians 10:4–5. I recommend memorizing this passage, which describes the weapons of our warfare. These weapons are not carnal or physical, but they are mighty in the supernatural realm of God for pulling down strongholds. A stronghold is a fortress, a place where the enemy is holed up, a dwelling place.

Picture the enemy as if they were hornets, then imagine destroying their nest so that they scatter. That is the idea of spiritual

Remember that the whole idea of warfare is to expose the enemy so that he no longer has walls to hide behind.

warfare: You go to the enemy's stronghold and tear down their hiding place, exposing them so that they can no longer hide. The enemy is always trying to remain covert. Notice how most crime occurs at night, in the darkness—you get the idea. Pulling down strongholds is also like when the walls of Jericho fell, exposing the enemy within them; this is a visual image of what happens when you cast down arguments or thoughts that rise up against the knowledge of God.

DISMANTLE STRONGHOLDS WITH TRUTH

And you shall know the truth, and the truth will set you free.

—John 8:32 NLT

Remember that the whole idea of warfare is to expose the enemy so that he no longer has walls to hide behind. If you want successful deliverance in people, you must teach it this way. In a service, when you dismantle the enemy by exposing him and people no longer have strongholds in their minds, deliverance will flow in the room. This reveals the enemy, which means you can anticipate deliverance in every Warrior Notes service. I do not have to address the devil or pull people out. I just preach the gospel. As I speak the truth, it addresses and dismantles the enemy's strongholds in people.

When He had been baptized, Jesus came up immediately from the water; and behold, the heavens were opened to Him, and He saw the Spirit of God descending like a dove and alighting upon Him. And suddenly a voice came from heaven, saying, "This is My beloved Son, in whom I am well pleased."

—Matthew 3:16–17

I would address people's arguments about certain truths during services by explaining them with Scripture. For example, some do not believe in the Trinity of the Godhead. When you look at Matthew 3, the scenario where John the Baptist baptized Jesus, you can see that denying the Trinity is a ridiculous lie. When John baptized Jesus, the Holy Spirit descended on Him. Then the Father God spoke from Heaven saying, "This is my beloved Son, in whom I am well pleased." That voice was the God of Abraham, Isaac, and Jacob. The God and Father of our Lord Jesus Christ spoke from Heaven while Jesus was on earth as the Son being baptized; Jesus did not throw His voice up into the air and say that; the Father was speaking.

Just to drive the point home—the Father speaks from His throne while the Spirit of God is descending on Jesus, who was being baptized. How could we deny the Trinity? That is only one of many examples. I just cast down an argument. How? I stated the truth of the Bible. We are all called to speak the truth.

> **When we come against the doctrinal issues, the lies of the enemy in people's minds, then those associated demons have to leave.**

Through Warrior Notes, people are sent out to preach the gospel. They are not just going out; they are being sent. You are already ordained by God, and He will honor your faithfulness. You are called to preach the favorable year of the Lord—the year of Jubilee—and to cast down strongholds by teaching Scripture.

The strategy of demons is to exalt themselves above the knowledge of God. They want to deceive people because they know anyone who accepts their lies will be robbed of God's favor. They seek to get people to sin and walk away from God, which happened with Adam and Eve. They had to be tricked into deception. The serpent brought an argument to confuse Eve concerning what God said. He tried to make it sound like God was holding back from them when He was not (Genesis 3:1–7). This is real spiritual warfare.

When we come against the doctrinal issues, the lies of the enemy in people's minds, then those associated demons have to leave. People do not have demons in their spirits, but unclean spirits are around them, influencing their souls; they are being held captive.

Once you explain to them that God did not cause the traumatic events that allowed these demons to enter and get them to forgive and be healed, the demons leave because they have no stronghold left. We are supposed to destroy their strongholds; that's the bottom line.

> *You will tread on the lion and the adder; the young lion and the serpent you will trample underfoot.*
>
> —Psalm 91:13 ESV

In Luke 10:18–19, Jesus said He saw satan fall like lightning from Heaven. He continued by stating that He gave believers authority to tread on serpents and scorpions. Jesus promised that you would have power over all the enemy and that nothing would injure or harm us. In this passage, Jesus was quoting from Psalm 91. Verse 13 states that you will tread on the lion and the adder—some translations say serpent, scorpion, the young lion, and the dragon (which is the serpent)—and you shall trample them underfoot. Psalm 91:10 says that no evil or disease can come near you.

Jesus was paraphrasing this when He said, "Nothing shall be any means hurt you" in Luke 10:19. So He took what He learned from the Old Testament as a boy and quoted it. He transferred that revelation to the New Testament and taught that by invoking His name, we would see demons driven out of people and trampled on. We have the authority to tread on serpents and scorpions and have power over the enemy.

TRIUMPH THROUGH THE CROSS

When He had disarmed the rulers and author-ities [those supernatural forces of evil operating against us], He made a public example of them [exhibiting them as captives in His triumphal procession], having triumphed over them through the cross.

—Colossians 2:15 AMP

When Jesus disarmed the rulers and authorities, He made a public display of them, having triumphed over them through the cross (Colossians 2:15). Paul uses words to describe the levels of evil spirits in Ephesians 6, which we discussed. When Jesus went to the cross and triumphed over them, He bought us back; however, only those who believe through Jesus Christ are saved (Romans 10:9–10). Jesus defeated and judged all these evil spirits, rulers, and authorities but did not remove them—they are still there. He embarrassed them by making a public spectacle of them. That is the truth from the Word of God on which we stand.

When driving unclean spirits out of people, Jesus did not do what we see today in deliverance ministries, such as sending demons to the pit. I am not going to do anything that Jesus did not do. As we discussed, I will certainly not go outside my boundaries because that will invite trouble.

> *And Moses said to the people, "Do not be afraid. Stand still, and see the salvation of the Lord, which He will accomplish for you today. For the Egyptians whom you see today, you shall see again no more forever. The Lord will fight for you, and you shall hold your peace."*
>
> —Exodus 14:13–14

Another Scripture that I recommend memorizing is the previous passage, Exodus 14:13–14. This passage tells us not to be afraid. We are to stand still and see the salvation of the Lord, who will fight for us. This is another confirmation of what Paul expressed in Ephesians 6 about standing firm and being still. I believe Paul got his revelation from this passage in Exodus. As a Pharisee, he knew the Old Testament well, but the New Testament was not written yet. The idea here is that the Lord has already given us victory and endowed us with all the weapons we need. Our armor is defensive; therefore, the Lord will execute our victory by fighting for us. These verses do not say we are supposed to initiate a fight; we are instructed to stand. The Lord will fight your battles, so hold your peace and stand still.

You must understand the correction that as the church, we are not obtaining something—we already have it. Now, we are defending and protecting what we were given. The way Paul approaches this is vastly different from what is being portrayed as spiritual warfare today. Many people encounter backlash and negative experiences from attempting spiritual battles because they are not staying within the proper boundaries or respecting authority. Many also lack understanding regarding what Jesus accomplished for humanity through the cross.

As mentioned several times, individuals can drive out the earthbound demons, the serpents, and the scorpions that Luke 10:19 refers to. Even though Jesus triumphed over the higher entities on the cross, these must only be dealt with through the local church as the Holy Spirit leads.

BIBLICAL MINISTRY

Biblical ministry begins with the sending of an apostle into an area. Once that apostle is established there, they start a work. The prophet co-labors with the apostle by speaking from the other realm, giving insight, and opening up the heavenly realms. Then, the evangelist goes into the community and gathers people to hear the gospel message. At that point, teachers and pastors are set over the local body; pastors can also be teachers.

Once a work is established, the apostle continues to go out, starting new works. Then the prophet comes in, opening up the heavens and prophesying the word of the Lord, which will involve the will of God for that area. And then the evangelist again goes into the streets, gathering people, telling them about Jesus, and bringing them in. Once they hear the gospel message and are saved, pastors and teachers collaborate locally to mentor and disciple them. This process repeats itself as they continue to expand. This is how warfare should be going on locally; it is the order God set up, and I wish it were followed more because it is so simple.

Warfare and deliverance are very easy to understand. As the body of Christ, we must get back on track and stick to the proper course established for us.

What did the Holy Spirit reveal to you regarding this chapter?

_____

_____

_____

_____

_____

_____

_____

_____

_____

_____

CHAPTER 6

OLD TESTAMENT FRAMEWORK FOR DELIVERANCE

*For the Lord your God is He who
goes with you, to fight for you against
your enemies, to save you.*

—Deuteronomy 20:4

I hope that by now, you have a better understanding of your enemy and what you are contending with. I believe that knowing what demons really are and their mode of operation has already simplified deliverance for you.

The revelations I received when I was with Jesus in Heaven concerning spiritual warfare were clearly defined in Scripture, but honestly, I had not previously heard much teaching about it. I realized that most people were just as much in the dark as I was about this topic. The Lord showed me that if I would seek out the treasure of Scripture, I would find the truth about everything. In the chapters ahead, we will continue to build upon the foundation that has been laid by examining more Scriptures.

As mentioned, New Testament leaders, including Jesus Himself, were educated in the old covenant through the Old Testament Scriptures. Jesus was brought up as a Jewish boy who had to memorize Scripture because that was part of their culture (Luke 2:46–47). Likewise, Paul was a Pharisee who was an expert in the law (Philippians 3:4–5). He was a theologian who understood the Old Testament, inside and out. Paul supernaturally received revelation from Jesus Christ; however, all the New Testament Scripture was still being written. The point is that you will often see references from the Old Testament in the writings of the New Testament. Even many of Jesus's teachings include almost word-for-word quotes from the Old Testament.

GOD FIGHTS FOR YOU AND ESTABLISHES YOUR PATH

We must never forget that we are not fighting on our own. As we previously discussed, Jesus was sent to do the Father's will and encountered the enemy on the way; He never sought out warfare or the devil. Demons manifested themselves on the way and talked to Him. The framework for this understanding can be observed in the Old Testament. When the Lord would speak to Moses or the prophets and the people obeyed His word, God would fight their enemies and give them victory. For example, in Deuteronomy 20:1–4, the Lord told Moses that when Israel had to go to battle, the troops should not be afraid because the Lord their God would go with them, giving them victory over their enemies.

> *Let no one say when he is tempted, "I am tempted of God"; for God cannot be tempted by evil, neither tempteth he any man: but every man is tempted, when he is drawn away of his own lust, and enticed. Then, when lust hath conceived, it bringeth forth sin; and sin, when it is finished, bringeth forth death.*
>
> —James 1:13–15 KJV

We must never forget that we are not fighting on our own.

The mindset of the New Testament is not going out to fight a physical battle but understanding that the Lord is with us; our warfare and the weapons God gave us are spiritual. The demonic entities that we wrestle with manifest themselves through people. They gain access to individuals by infiltrating their thoughts, changing their minds, and influencing their desires. If left unchecked, they will eventually deceive their victims and trick them into sinning as the serpent did to Adam and Eve. Once they sin, the enemy has an open door to trap them in bondage. When people are deceived or convinced of lies, demons then put shackles on them. At that point, they are demonized and need help.

Demonized people need the message of the gospel preached to them and to have the demons cast out of them; in other words, they need deliverance. Just as God defeated the physical enemies of His people in the Old Testament, through Jesus Christ, He has given us victory over the demonic.

I waited patiently for the Lord; and He inclined unto me, and heard my cry. He brought me up also out of an horrible pit, out of the miry clay, and set my feet upon a rock, and established my goings. And He hath put a new song in my mouth, even praise unto our God: many shall see it, and fear, and shall trust in the Lord.

—Psalm 40:1–3 KJV

The psalmist testified that God delivered him when he cried out to the Lord and waited patiently for Him. Essentially, the lesson that we learn here is that we stand. As it says in Ephesians 6, when we have done everything, we must stand and wait patiently, knowing that God will incline His ear and hear us. We must be confident that the Lord will answer and pull us out of the pit.

Picture the miry clay, like quicksand, where your feet get stuck. Envision the Lord pulling you out of that and setting you on a solid foundation, the rock in this passage. Know that God will establish your goings; in other words, God ordained a clear pathway for you, which He will set you on.

God is faithful to make your pathway obvious so you will not miss it. One of the goals of this book is to show you that there is a set path for you. When you are in a forest with an established pathway, it is so clear that going off the trail is difficult. That means it's well-used and well-defined, which is why I called this book Deliverance Made Easy.

When I encountered Jesus in Heaven, I was shown my life and the messages I was supposed to teach. He clearly gave me the topics, which is why you hear all this revelation from Warrior Notes. For forty-five minutes, Jesus stood with me and taught me the Scriptures; however, it seemed like a week of teaching. I was undergoing an operation that was less than an hour, but it seemed like I was gone much longer because there were no clocks in Heaven or references to time. It just seemed like it went on and on and on. He established me on the pathway of my life. It was so well-defined that when I came back, it took a long time to convince me that what I was shown had not physically happened yet.

After I visited Heaven, I endured warfare for years. I suffered many hardships until 2016, when I recorded my first show on Sid Roth. Shortly afterward, in 2017, I retired from Southwest Airlines. During that time, I had many physical problems, especially my sinuses and ears, so that I could barely fly. The pain was indescribable.

Many realities I experienced in Heaven had not happened when I returned to earth, even though I knew they were true. There was such a struggle at times. It took many years for me to process what happened during my visitation in 1992. I could not write the book Heavenly Visitation until 2015. I published it in 2016 and then was on TV. It took a lot of time for what I was shown to be integrated into my mind and into my physical body.

Other supernatural events happened to me, just like they probably have to you. God answered prayers and moved in my life. Yet I could only dream of the revelation of God's plans shown to me being fulfilled in my life, although I knew they were true. Much of it slipped from my memory after a while, so when I wrote the book, it helped to bring it all back to the forefront.

I shared my journey to show you that I had to go through a process where God had to manifest my deliverance and come through for me. From 1992 through 2015, the Lord worked the revelations into my life. In 2016, I started to be established in all these truths. A war went on just to write that first book, which took me a year and a half. All I was doing was documenting what the Lord taught me on the other side and what happened in my heavenly visitation. You would think that would be an easy task, but I dealt with so much warfare that I struggled to sit down and write. The devil did not want that book to come out and certainly did not want me on TV. Essentially, he has tried to undermine everything concerning Warrior Notes every step of the way.

The Lord established my goings, just as it says in Scripture. He put a song in my mouth to give praise unto God. I was pulled out of a horrible pit, shown the right way to live in Heaven, and sent back to earth. Many people have seen what God has done and how I have trusted in the Lord. Because of this, they have become acquainted with Warrior Notes and me. The testimony of Psalm 40 truly happened to me. The fruit of it all is that the deliverance that God did for me has become part of the experience of people around me. That is what will happen to you too.

I believe you will experience the Lord's strong arm in your life; it will be just as powerful and effective for you as it was for me. God will come through for you. You will be acquainted with His power and the deliverance of His arm grabbing you and pulling you out. Then, you will see the enemy leave very quickly. He will vacate when you show up because you have already gained victory. When the Lord has won you over, the enemy knows it and flees.

THE ENEMY FLEES FROM THOSE WHO HAVE SIDED WITH GOD

Let God arise, let His enemies be scattered; Let those also who hate Him flee before Him. As smoke is driven away, so drive them away; As

wax melts before the fire, so let the wicked per-
ish at the presence of God. But let the righteous
be glad; Let them rejoice before God; Yes, let
them rejoice exceedingly.

— Psalm 68:1–3

Another aspect of the framework of how deliverance worked among the people of the Old Testament is found in Psalm 68:1–3. The God of the Old Testament is the same God of the New Testament. The New Testament was written from the Old with Jesus being the fulfillment (Matthew 5:17). The Holy Spirit implemented the covenant that Jesus cut through His blood (Hebrews 10:15–18).

I encourage you to meditate on these Scriptures, building up your frame of mind, and you will effortlessly see deliverance happen not only in your own life but in the lives of others. You will not even have to fast or pray necessarily. I am not saying that fasting and prayer are not important; these are necessary for every believer. However, you should be thoroughly convinced and understand the ways of God, knowing that He will arise and scatter His enemies, which are your enemies. This is God's way of life, not something you must obtain by doing something special. Psalm 68:1 says to let those who hate God flee before Him. You will see that happen when any demons attack your life.

When you have taken sides with God, the enemy that hates God will hate you too. You should not take it personally. The Scripture says that when this happens, the enemy will become like smoke that is just driven away and like wax that melts before the fire. The psalmist describes what will happen to your adversaries, who are also God's enemies. He said, "Let the wicked perish at the presence of God." The righteous, which is you and me, will be glad and rejoice before God exceedingly. We will see the victory.

You should build yourself up by meditating on these Scriptures. Then you will see God deliver people because the enemy knows you are thoroughly convinced. He will vacate because he knows he has to leave. With this revelation, you do not need to consider yourself a deliverance minister. Demons manifest when you become established in who you are in the Spirit. When you understand what God has done in you, you become settled in it, and the enemy opts out of the battle. With Jesus, demons knew they had to leave, so they just said, "Are you going to torment us before our time?" They did not argue whether or not they would have to leave. They already knew they would have to, but they did not want to be sent to the pit or out of their assigned area (Mark 5:10).

Demonic spirits have worked hard to develop a network in each neighborhood, city, state, and country. It messes everything up when you encounter strongmen and send them out of the area. When you address them, it sets them back, sometimes years, in the process of what they have been doing in that city. As the body of Christ, we want to do this as much as possible.

The demons tried to negotiate with Jesus because they were doing damage control. Scripture does not say He sent them out of the area; however, it also does not say you cannot do so. You cannot send them to torment until it is their time (Matthew 8:29); the defined time appears to be at the end of this age when the angel comes and throws satan into the lake of fire (Revelation 20:10).

The enemy is already judged up until that point; we are supposed to be enforcing the victory that we have through Jesus Christ by driving them out. So we can drive them out of their territory or domain. The Bible does not say we cannot do that. The boundary is that we cannot send them to the pit to be tormented before their time. It is essential to rehearse these Scriptures.

THE CHURCH'S RESPONSIBILITY

Thine hand shall be lifted up upon thine adversaries, and all thine enemies shall be cut off.

—Micah 5:9 KJV

We know that what is said in the Old Testament is truth. However, the revelation about Jesus, His fulfillment, and His implementation of the new covenant builds upon this truth. Jesus Christ fulfilled the demands of the Old Testament and the law. Understand that through Him, we have victory over all our adversaries, and the enemy shall be cut off. I want to assure you that we can cut off the demons' strength and ability to operate.

In every area, the church is responsible for cutting off the enemy. Whether a body of believers gathering in a house or a building, we agree to break up the enemy's supply in specific geographic regions and cut off their communication. We can command confusion to come into the enemy's camp (Psalm 55:9).

You can stop the demons' supply by starving them. Do not give them any response or satisfaction, which would allow them to grow. Disembodied spirits gain power by feeding off people's souls. You starve them by preventing them from having any satisfaction or fulfillment by being close to a human being. When demons do not have a human host, they go into arid places and suffer. That is why they are seeking a body where they can live. Instead, send them to arid areas where they dry up.

Understand that through Him, we have victory over all our adversaries, and the enemy shall be cut off.

What did the Holy Spirit reveal to you regarding this chapter?

_____

_____

_____

_____

_____

_____

_____

_____

_____

_____

_____

_____

_____

_____

_____

_____

_____

_____

_____

_____

CHAPTER 7

JESUS PAID FOR YOUR FREEDOM

*And it shall come to pass in that day,
that his burden shall be taken away
from off thy shoulder, and his yoke
from off thy neck, and the yoke shall be
destroyed because of the anointing.*
—Isaiah 10:27 KJV

I n the New Testament, Jesus fulfilled many Old Testament prophecies, including those Isaiah declared concerning the Messiah. We need to memorize and meditate on these powerful Scriptures, some of which we will discuss in this chapter. We must let them become part of us because they will help us fight the enemy so that we may see people delivered.

THE GOSPEL IS GIVEN FREELY

As you read and study the revelation in this chapter, I believe you will experience your deliverance. The anointing and power of impartation are here, and demons must leave you alone. However, that is not the only goal; you are called to operate in this same anointing wherever you go so that the enemy screams, gives up, and leaves before you even say anything. The ultimate goal for Warrior Notes Ministry is discipleship.

> *Heal the sick, cleanse the lepers, raise the dead, cast out demons. Freely you received, freely give.*
>
> —Matthew 10:8

Just to be clear, I want to see you completely delivered. My desire is that the enemy leaves your life and no longer has any power over you. You are meant to walk in the victory that Jesus has given us. However, the fruit of this would be for you to turn around and do the same thing for others, which is what the church is supposed to be doing. As the body and church of the Lord Jesus Christ, we are supposed to operate in His authority on earth, which means we should drive out demons as He did. It is straightforward.

Isaiah 10:27 tells us that the anointing will destroy yokes and burdens. Jesus Christ is the Anointed One, so the burdens and yokes are removed when He shows up. This means you will not have to carry them anymore. Sometimes when people experience a breakthrough, they feel the manifestation of a weight lift off their shoulders. When a yoke is destroyed, it can never be fixed or put back on you—it is permanent.

What bothers me the most about some of today's so-called deliverance ministries is that people must pay to attend their meetings to get delivered. People have told me that they have been charged to listen to spiritual warfare seminars and then had to pay extra for deliverance prayer. Some ministers charge additional fees for personal deliverance sessions. I disassociate myself from all ministers and ministries that charge, and there are many.

You should never feel pressured to give an offering, as if under coercion, even to meet a ministry's expenses (2 Corinthians 9:7). Warrior Notes will never pressure people to give, even if we have costs. I tell everybody that the partners have already paid for the conferences and other ministries because I want to remove that pressure from those attending. I would never want anyone to give because they felt forced to do so; that completely goes against Scripture.

Sadly, some ministries manipulate people to increase offerings. Even though some might not charge at the door (which many do), if they let you in for free, they emphasize how much the meeting costs. They may phrase it as raising funds, but to me, it is just like charging. I have been in meetings where they prolong the offering so that people feel compelled to give just to get on with the service. I have seen some practices I do not think any apostles or biblical leaders would ever approve of.

> *What is my reward then? That when I preach the gospel, I may present the gospel of Christ*

without charge, that I may not abuse my authority in the gospel.

—1 Corinthians 9:18

Everything that we have been given through Jesus Christ was provided without charge. It was costly to Jesus and the Father, so it was not free; however, the gospel was given at no cost. Paul did accept offerings, but he said that we should not give out of manipulation. Nobody should be coerced into giving; we should want to do it out of joy.

God loves a cheerful giver, according to 2 Corinthians 8 and 9. These are not very popular chapters of the Bible. These passages teach that you do not have to give if you do not want to; you should give only out of joy and for the right reasons.

DELIVERANCE IS PERMANENT

The anointing removes and destroys demonic yokes. The anointing cannot be bought or manipulated; God freely gives it, and it is permanent. However, regardless of whether or not you paid for it, you should be delivered permanently. Amazingly, many have been charged for deliverance seminars and even paid extra for the materials and prayer to find that their freedom was not permanent. Some people will do anything to be delivered—even pay significant sums—then when you talk to them, the demons have come back.

The anointing on the Messiah and given to us, the body of Christ, is the yoke-destroying anointing. I must emphasize and repeat this because God said that on the day of the Messiah, which is now, the yoke will be removed from our necks and destroyed because of the anointing. The anointing is the Anointed One—the Messiah, the Deliverer, period. Jesus gave deliverance for free, and it is permanent. So if the ministry we received is temporary, we must look at what is really going on. The problem is that people must be taught the simplicity of deliverance and understand that God is with them.

> *No man shall be able to stand before you all the days of your life; as I was with Moses, so I will be with you. I will not leave you or forsake you.*
>
> —Joshua 1:5–6

Since God is with you, your enemies are now His enemies. They will not be able to stand before Him. When you invoke the name of Jesus, use the power of His blood, and talk about the covenant, demons will leave because there is no contest (Mark 16:17). Jesus always offered permanent—not temporary—deliverance.

The demons understood that He was sent and knew why He was on earth; they asked Him, "Have you come to destroy us before our time?" Jesus did destroy the works of the enemy on the cross, so now it is finished (1 John 3:8; John 19:30). Now that the works of the enemy

> **Through Him, there will never be a time when a demon does not leave. The Person who is our God never takes no for an answer.**

have been destroyed, all we are doing is showing up as ambassadors. The point is that we do not have to spend a whole weekend and pay a lot of money to learn deliverance.

At times, it is appropriate to charge for a service. For example, we charge a small cost at the Warrior Notes School of Ministry for those who can pay because it is a legitimate university degree. It is appropriate to charge for college credit because we have to pay our staff to run the school. The courses, which include technology, are done with excellence, and it costs money to do that. I spent hundreds and hundreds of dollars per credit hour for my degree, but I ensure that never happens for our students at the School of Ministry. We keep the costs very minimal, so it is affordable.

When you receive ministry to be delivered from demonic oppression, it should be free and permanent, which is not happening with most ministries today, so I need to address it. God has promised permanent deliverance through the anointing of the Holy One, the Messiah. When you meet Him, He will tell you His blood was enough. Through Him, there will never be a time when a demon does not leave. The Person who is our God never takes no for an answer. I know this to be true because I met Jesus and talked to Him before I was sent back. If He says something, it is established and will come to pass.

Jesus will have His way. If you are in the way, He will move you out of the way. You will be asked to step aside if you do not side with Him. That is just how Jesus is; He will tell you that His blood was enough. You will not go to Jesus and say to Him that you commanded a demon to leave and it would not listen to the name of Jesus. You cannot make the excuse that it did not obey; it will not happen. You will not say, "It did not work," because Jesus will tell you, "My blood was enough. My name is enough." He would tell you that He is not returning to be crucified again. There is nothing more He can do.

> So when Jesus had received the sour wine, He said, "It is finished!" And bowing His head, He gave up His spirit.
>
> —John 19:30

When Jesus hung on the cross, right before He died, He said, "It is finished." The word He spoke was tetelestai,[7] which means "paid in full"; there are no amendments and nothing left to do about the enemy.

---

7. "G5055 - *teleō* - Strong's Greek Lexicon," Blue Letter Bible, accessed July 23, 2023, https://www.blueletterbible.org/lexicon/g5055/nkjv/tr/0-1/.

Jesus's death on the cross has legally processed the transaction. Every covenant promise in the Bible has already been paid; the cost to get the message to you was significant. Yet a requirement to make people pay for it is wrong; you cannot do that if you are sent.

Demons love it when you overemphasize them. They also love it when you charge for something that should be free. Some expenses are understandable, but you should not be paying for your deliverance or prayer. The same applies to every aspect of the gospel, yet deliverance ministry has been severely abused in this way.

I want to know why people are being charged for ministry. If God has sent you, He will bless and prosper you and pay for it supernaturally. Jesus did not charge, yet He did take offerings. He had a money bag, which had a lot of money in it (John 13:29). The money had to get into the bag somehow. The Bible does not explicitly say, but it is implied that some individuals followed Jesus around and financed Him. Later, others financed the apostles too. This is God's way of doing it.

> When you pass through the waters, I will be with you; And through the rivers, they shall not overflow you. When you walk through the fire, you shall not be burned, nor shall the flame scorch you.
>
> —Isaiah 43:2

Isaiah 43:2 states that God guarantees protection from the enemy for His people. Whether it is water or fire, you will be completely protected. We must have this mindset when encountering the enemy; it is the whole idea of Psalm 91.

> *"No weapon that is formed against you will succeed; And every tongue that rises against you in judgment you will condemn. This [peace, righteousness, security, and triumph over opposition] is the heritage of the servants of the Lord, and this is their vindication from Me," says the Lord.*
>
> —Isaiah 54:17 AMP

I also recommend memorizing Isaiah 54:17. This verse says that anything the enemy manufactures to come against you will not prosper or succeed. Every person who speaks a lie or a judgment against you will be condemned. Here, the prophet Isaiah prophesied about the future. All these promises are the heritage of the Lord's servants. So your deliverance and everything that you get from God is free. If something is your heritage, it means that you inherit it freely. In this verse, the Lord says that He will vindicate you.

TRAFFICKING DEMONS

I have watched many deliverance sessions from different individuals, and it took a while to discern what was going on. I witnessed one case where I thought the ministry was legitimate, but I eventually discerned a familiar spirit in operation. Some of these individuals claiming to minister deliverance were, in fact, trafficking demons—people were not really being delivered. I saw genuine manifestations, but then suddenly, the demons jumped from one person to another. The so-called minister operated as a master of ceremonies, trafficking the demons so that they manifested and appeared as if they were being cast out.

I repeatedly watched these deliverance videos and clearly saw the demons going from one person to another. The Lord called this a revolving door. In other words, the same thing keeps happening. These meetings took place at large churches in different countries; they emphasized deliverance, but it was more like voodoo or a séance. They repeatedly trafficked demons through revolving doors in the spirit realm.

Many deliverance ministries are a scam and work with familiar spirits. I found out later that many of these ministers were previously involved in witchcraft ceremonies. You would probably know all these people. Through these ceremonies, they were initiated and given supernatural powers from demons that cooperated to put on a show. I was surprised because I was initially deceived; I thought they were legitimate until I could not ignore that something was wrong. I checked into it with local ministers and pastors in those countries to find that everyone had the same story.

I exposed what occurs in many deliverance ministries because the enemy wants to deceive people; he does not want you to know the truth about him. For the devil to have power, he has to hide the truth. Many things are happening today that we call ministry, but it is not the ministry of the Holy Spirit. It does not seem like anybody is speaking up about it. However, I will do what the Lord tells me to do. I want you to be aware of fraudulent ministry so that you can let the Lord speak to you; it does not have to take you as long as it took me to figure this out.

I have distanced myself from many ministries because they are operating in familiar spirits. Sometimes, the ministers who seem to get promoted on TV are not doing well spiritually, but you would not know it. Their ministries are a revolving door, creating the appearance of deliverance.

In the book of Acts, Paul dealt with familiar spirits in people followed him. In Acts 16:16–18, a woman acted like she was promoting the gospel by telling the crowds to listen to these men (Paul and Silas) tell them the way to salvation. Perhaps he initially thought something was

For the devil to have power, he has to hide the truth.

wrong but did not address it for several days. After three days, Paul heard clearly from the Lord that this was not the Holy Spirit but a familiar spirit in operation. At that point, he addressed that demon and cast it out. That demon had been trying to preserve its position in her and the city.

If you look at what happened, that lady had brought great wealth to businesspeople, so they got mad when she lost her power (Acts 16:19–24). They wanted the apostles to leave the city because of the so-called damage they had done, so the city turned against them because they negatively impacted their finances.

> *For the love of money [that is, the greedy desire for it and the willingness to gain it unethically] is a root of all sorts of evil, and some by longing for it have wandered away from the faith and pierced themselves [through and through] with many sorrows.*
>
> —1 Timothy 6:10 AMP

When you investigate many ministries today, you will discover they are centered on making money. That is why you will see them charging and pushing offerings. This information will help you discern which ministries are doing this. I desire for you to develop your understanding in the area of deliverance for yourself and other people. I want you to have a firm foundation of what the Word of God says and be aware that the enemy does not want ministers operating in deliverance the right way. He is going to attack ministers and ministries in an attempt to render them ineffective. I am making it very simple so you can discern and see clearly.

What did the Holy Spirit reveal to you regarding this chapter?

_____

_____

_____

_____

_____

_____

_____

_____

_____

_____

_____

_____

_____

_____

_____

_____

_____

_____

_____

_____

CHAPTER 8

THE BATTLE IS
ALREADY WON

*The Lord thy God in the midst of thee is
mighty; He will save, He will rejoice over
thee with joy; He will rest in His love,
He will joy over thee with singing.*
—Zephaniah 3:17 KJV

We discussed the enemy's corruption of deliverance ministry with money and began uncovering his mode of operation through familiar spirits disguised as ministry of the Holy Spirit. I have noticed that many ministers have taken on these spirits, so you must be careful these days and understand that there should not be an overemphasis on deliverance or any one aspect of the gospel. I will continue to expose how the enemy works behind the scenes in the light of God's truth so that you can recognize his schemes and avoid pitfalls.

> *The Spirit of the Lord God is upon Me, because the Lord has anointed Me to preach good tidings to the poor; He has sent Me to heal the brokenhearted, to proclaim liberty to the captives, and the opening of the prison to those*

who are bound; to proclaim the acceptable year
of the Lord, and the day of vengeance of our
God; to comfort all who mourn.

—Isaiah 61:1–2

We are called to preach and demonstrate the gospel message described in Isaiah 61:1–2 just like Jesus did. Deliverance is just one of the different aspects of the gospel message. As you walk with the Lord, Isaiah 54:17 promises that no weapon formed against you will prosper and your vindication will come from the Lord. In light of this truth, we must recognize the weapons of the enemy when they form, especially the ones that come disguised as blessings from God.

A TRANSACTION WITH THE DEVIL

To keep satan from taking advantage of us; for
we are not ignorant of his schemes.

—2 Corinthians 2:11 AMP

As previously discussed, Paul had to separate himself from the woman following him (Acts 16:16–19). She promoted their ministry by saying, "Listen, these people are of God." However, she was a witch who, in reality, was masking a familiar spirit, hoping that Paul would not cast it out. That evil spirit knew that Paul went from city to city, so perhaps it was hoping to lie low and act like a supporter until he left. It wanted to stay in that woman and continue to collect money for fortune telling.

Fortune telling is performed by witches who traffic familiar spirits. People come to them and pay to have their future told. It works because the evil spirits obtain information from the spirit realm for the witches to tell their clients. These demons get information from familiar spirits who know the person's family. The clients are often amazed when a fortune teller reveals something about them that a stranger would never know. Afterward, the witch says something about the future to hook the person and inserts some curse to ensnare them. For example, they may tell them that the same disease that killed their father will come upon them unless they deal with it. Then, the scared person pays the witch to eliminate this curse and prevent the prediction from happening.

When you pay a fortune teller or a witch, a transaction takes place. In other words, if you offer money

> **We are called to preach and demonstrate the gospel message described in Isaiah 61:1–2 just like Jesus did. Deliverance is just one of the different aspects of the gospel message.**

to deal with an evil spirit to prevent something terrible from happening, you have unknowingly made an agreement with the demonic realm; this opens the door to their influence in other ways. You would not think that witchcraft could creep into the church; however, these transactions with witches and warlocks happen thousands of times per day where people pay and go through the process I just described.

Familiar spirits stand beside mediums who are witches or warlocks; these spirits go and get information, come back at the speed of light, and give the information to the witch. When the witches share it with their clients, they are surprised. When they are open, the witch may say something futuristic or give a fortune; then, they will share bad news concerning what is working against them. People often fall right into the trap and pay the witch or warlock to prevent the curse; however, they unknowingly made a deal with the devil, which may seem good initially but never ends well. This often happens in Hollywood and is why many people rise into what they call stardom and are later struck with tragedy.

I have seen a disturbing trend of witchcraft creeping into the church, especially among the prophetic and deliverance ministries. Have you noticed that when there are meetings with several guest prophets, you must pay to get in? Some are so bold that you have to pay if you want a word or a preferred seat where you might get a word or to have a meal with the man or woman of God. This seems to be common among specific sectors. It mainly has to do with getting words and deliverance. These ministers work in the same ways that witches work. You can pay a witch or warlock to work with the familiar spirits to accomplish anything you want, whether good or bad. Sadly, more people do not see through this.

> *And when Simon saw that through the laying on of the apostles' hands the Holy Spirit was given, he offered them money, saying, "Give me this power also, that anyone on whom I lay hands may receive the Holy Spirit." But Peter said to him, "Your money perish with you, because you thought that the gift of God could be purchased with money! You have neither part nor portion in this matter, for your heart is not right in the sight of God. Repent therefore of this your wickedness, and pray God if perhaps the thought of your heart may be forgiven you. For I see that you are poisoned by bitterness and bound by iniquity."*
>
> —Acts 8:18–23

Jesus, Paul, and the apostles never took money for preferred seating, words, or deliverance. Nobody in the Bible ever paid to get demons cast out. Simon was a warlock who offered to pay the apostles for the power to lay hands on people to receive the Holy Spirit. The apostle Peter said, "Your money perish with you!" In other words, he told Simon that he would be destroyed with his money. That might not have sounded very nice, but that is how it was. Can you imagine if I said that today?

FREELY DELIVERED
THROUGH CHRIST

Nobody wants to admit they are wrong. Many will find out they are wrong when they reach Heaven, but why wait? This is what happened to me. I was wrong about many things; therefore, when I got to Heaven, I was corrected. Although I had Bibles everywhere in my house, I was supernaturally given the word of God. The Lord showed me that He fights our enemies; He has already defeated the devil, so essentially, He has broken the bondage of the yoke off everybody. Now, captives are set free by preaching the gospel message and proclaiming this liberty. Deliverance comes through the gospel, not by charging people for counseling, prayer, or words.

Scripture does not say that deliverance comes from laying on of hands; it says that you lay hands on the sick, and they will recover (Mark 16:17–18). It does not say, "Lay hands on the demon-possessed, and they shall be delivered." Many processes are taking place in ministry that are contrary to how the Bible teaches. If the enemy is defeated but still influences people, we should look at what is really happening.

Ministries that charge for deliverance do not seem to have permanent results; as previously mentioned, it is a revolving door. It is the same with a prophetic ministry where many have paid to meet with a prophet, yet most of the so-called predictions did not come to pass. The people just ended up out of money.

Again, none of the apostles charged. In fact, they did not have prayer or prophecy lines; they did not call people out either. These practices developed in recent years; they were not part of the original church. They laid hands on and prayed for the sick, but mostly the elders did that (James 5:14–15), not the fivefold ministers. The book of Acts mentions a waiter named Stephen, who was not an apostle yet did notable miracles (Acts 6:2–8).

The bottom line is that deliverance has been given to us freely by Jesus Christ (Matthew 10:7–8); we are told to proclaim freedom to the captives (Luke 4:18–19). Just announce it—that declaration should shake up the enemy so that any demons start to vacate. And if a spirit manifests, so be it; however, we shouldn't look for a manifestation. I look for the exit that the enemy leaves through, preferring that he go quietly and never return—that is deliverance. The announcement of the gospel's good news makes demons uncomfortable with staying; that's the mindset of Scripture and what I want to teach you to do.

> *So they will fear the name of the Lord from the west and His glory from the rising of the sun. For He will come in like a narrow, rushing*

> stream which the breath of the Lord drives
> [overwhelming the enemy].

—Isaiah 59:19 AMP

Isaiah 59:19 says that when the enemy comes in, like a flood, the Spirit of the Lord will raise up a standard against him. Some translations are unclear, making it sound like the enemy is the one who pursues us like a flood; however, the Scripture states that when the enemy comes, the flood of the Spirit will come in and raise up a standard against that enemy. I want you to frame this right; in any situation you encounter, the Spirit of the Lord will raise up a standard. He will come in like a flood. Picture this—just as God flooded the earth to destroy the enemy in Genesis, He is flooding out your spiritual enemies. I encourage you to meditate on this revelation.

GOD IS A WARRIOR WHO SAVES

God wants to train all His people to speak by the Spirit, which is how everyone who believed in Jesus Christ spoke in the New Testament. Paul said everyone has a word, a psalm, a tongue, or an interpretation (1 Corinthians 14:26–33). He taught that it must be done in order with those seated in the congregation judging whether the words spoken are of God. With that in mind, if you knew that the entire assembly could say yay or nay, would you stand up and deliver what you feel you are supposed to say? Are you strong enough in your spirit about what you are about to say or do? Are you sure you would be able to withstand the judgment of the congregation? That is what Paul taught—everyone seated is to judge the words.

> *And the Lord shall utter His voice before His army: for His camp is very great: for He is strong that executeth His word: for the day of the Lord is great and very terrible; and who can abide it?*
>
> —Joel 2:11 KJV

I also recommend memorizing Joel 2:11. The heart of Warrior Notes is to train you to speak what the Spirit is saying, not what you think or feel. The Lord wants to speak through you as He utters His voice before His army.

I picture all of us as ministers who communicate what the Spirit says, addressing the army of God. When I speak, I am ministering to all of you chosen ones in the army of God. Even though I do not know everybody in the

The Scripture states that when the enemy comes, the flood of the Spirit will come in and raise up a standard against that enemy.

body of Christ on the earth now, as people join us, I am discovering how expansive it is. Hundreds of thousands of people worldwide have connected to Warrior Notes. A couple of years ago, we would have never known that so many people would be educated and discipled by the Spirit of God. He is bringing us together so that we will essentially utter what God is saying, fulfilling Joel's prophecy.

The Lord once said to me, "I am a warrior." I knew I had heard that in Scripture before and soon found it in Zephaniah 3:17. This verse declares that the Lord God is in the midst of you as a mighty, victorious warrior who will save you. He will rejoice over you with joy and quiet you in His love.

Zephaniah 3:17 is my favorite verse. The revelation from this verse inspired us to name the ministry Warrior Notes. The Lord sent someone to share the message of this verse with me when I first got saved. In 1982, when I was in my second year of college, an unknown individual knocked on my door. He claimed to be a student but was only there for one semester. I do not remember his name or previously seeing him, which was strange. I was fasting and praying when he knocked on the door. When I let him in, he stood there and told me the powerful message the Lord gave him.

He said, "I saw the enemy surrounding you. Then I saw the Lord come up to you. He was riding a white horse and handed you a stone with the phrase 'victorious warrior' on it. Then the Lord rode off." He shared his vision and prophetic word, then walked out. I never saw him again. Though I tried to find out his name, I could not locate him or find out anything about him. To this day, I do not know if he was actually a person or an angel.

I believe that the message from the mysterious student was how Warrior Notes came to be. The Lord is the ultimate warrior, and I knew Warrior Notes would be a story about victory. That was my white stone, which I later found written about in the Bible. Revelation 2:17 states that those who overcome are given a white stone with their new name on it. I later realized the depth of what this person shared with me when he saw the Lord hand me a white stone with the words victorious warrior.

I encourage you to study and meditate on Zephaniah 3:17. I want to emphasize that God will save you from your enemies; He will rejoice over you with joy and quiet or comfort you in His love. He has songs of joy that He sings over you; some translations call them "songs of deliverance." The Lord will sing songs of deliverance over you and around you, which is the flavor of what the young man saw in his vision. Armies of enemies were around me, which hemmed me in on every side. It did not look like I had a chance. Then the Lord handed me that stone, and that was the end of the enemy. The Lord had decreed that I would have victory over the enemy.

*Are not all the angels ministering spirits sent out
[by God] to serve (accompany, protect) those
who will inherit salvation? [Of course they are!]*

—Hebrews 1:14 AMP

The Lord reminded me of this encounter from college when I received my ministry, Warrior Notes, and wrote my first book. I realized that everything God did was tied to this vision that the young man shared with me. Then, I understood that the angels also had a part in my fulfillment of God's will. Angelic activity hinders satan and evil spirits. These mighty angels have often personally accompanied me and aided in ministry. Even as I share this revelation with you, angels surround me; the enemy does not stand a chance.

I noticed that when I am ministering, whether writing a book, filming, or teaching at a conference, these angels come and help rout the enemy. Sometimes demons just leave, even if I did not fast or address them as you would think. The angelic visitation somehow caused a deliverance. A person may fast or pray for deliverance, but sometimes, it does not happen as expected. It often comes through angelic activity.

What did the Holy Spirit reveal to you regarding this chapter?

_____

_____

_____

_____

_____

_____

_____

_____

_____

_____

_____

_____

_____

_____

_____

_____

_____

_____

_____

_____

_____

CHAPTER 9

THE LORD'S ANGELIC ARMY

O Lord God of Heaven's Armies! Where
is there anyone as mighty as You, O
Lord? You are entirely faithful.
—Psalm 89:8 NLT

We briefly discussed angelic activity in the last chapter and will continue to dive deeper into understanding how angels aid with deliverance. God can do what He wants but never goes against His Word. The Bible tells us how God established the realms with angels involved in warfare.

RETURN TO GOD'S MODE OF MINISTRY

Now when Joshua was by Jericho, he looked up,
and behold, a man was standing opposite him
with his drawn sword in his hand, and Joshua
went to him and said to him, "Are you for us
or for our adversaries?" He said, "No; rather
I have come now as captain of the army of the
Lord." Then Joshua fell with his face toward

the earth and bowed down, and said to him,
"What does my lord have to say to his servant?"

—Joshua 5:13–14 AMP

In Joshua 5, the angel of the Lord approached Joshua, who was already in warfare mode. When Joshua encountered this warrior on the road, he had just led the Israelites toward Jerusalem, conquering cities with hybrid giants. Joshua thought he was flesh and blood and was ready to fight as he asked, "Are you for us or against us?" He was not afraid because he was sent.

The angel of the Lord surprisingly replied, "Neither." He was completely neutral, neither for nor against anyone but came as the captain of the Lord's army. This profound statement shows that he was not taking sides with Joshua or anyone else; he was on the Lord's side and was also sent.

The Lord had sent His army to help but did not tell Joshua at first. The commander angel had to wait for God's instruction; however, it did not come through Joshua. Interestingly, we try to define everything and attempt to set up plans that do not work. Throughout church history, we have been trying to figure out the working mode for ministry, including deliverance. We have tried one method for a while, then switched to another. One moment, people are told to let go, then, in the next, they are instructed to hold on. Many deliverance ministries have people cough and do all these forced manifestations to try to make it work.

Like deliverance, ministries have devised many fleshly modes of getting people filled with the Holy Spirit. You should let the power of God come on a person and fill them with the Spirit; He does not need help. In the early church, ministers did not coerce people, pat them on the back, or tell them to speak a specific word in tongues. People have been filled with the Spirit and were not even instructed to speak in tongues. In several instances in the book of Acts, people were filled with the Spirit; in all but one occurrence, people started speaking in tongues. Only once does it not specify that they spoke in tongues, but it is implied that they did (Acts 8:15–17). In all the other passages, they clearly spoke in tongues when filled with the Spirit.

The apostles explained to people that they needed to be filled with the Spirit, which is a different experience than salvation. They were not told that they would speak in tongues—they just did, which makes it more profound (Acts 2:4; 10:44–46). So if people were filled with the Spirit without being told they needed to speak in tongues, why are ministries operating the way they do today?

Many deliverance ministers ask people to do and say unbiblical things. They even talk to the demons instead of those receiving ministry, pushing for a manifestation. In the Bible days, demons spoke up; they were so freaked out and frustrated by the presence of Jesus or those He sent out that they just manifested.

> Then the seventy returned with joy, saying, "Lord, even the demons are subject to us in

Your name." And He said to them, "I saw satan fall like lightning from heaven. Behold, I give you the authority to trample on serpents and scorpions, and over all the power of the enemy, and nothing shall by any means hurt you. Nevertheless do not rejoice in this, that the spirits are subject to you, but rather rejoice because your names are written in heaven."

—Luke 10:17–20

According to some translations, the seventy (or seventy-two) Jesus sent out in Luke 10 were surprised that the demons obeyed them. Jesus told them not to rejoice because of that but because their names were written in the Lamb's Book of Life. In other words, we are not supposed to focus on the fact that demons obey us; our focus should be on our salvation and that we are ambassadors. This passage is recorded because of the abuse Jesus knew would occur in the coming days.

I will not conjure up a manifestation or implement a mode of operation based on what the devil does because anything he says or does is a lie. You cannot trust what he says; he can quote Scripture better than you can and will try to twist God's Word. So you cannot depend on anything a demon says. Why would you want to talk to them if they are liars? Even if they did say something true, how would you know?

> *As each has received a gift, use it to serve one another, as good stewards of God's varied grace: whoever speaks, as one who speaks oracles of God; whoever serves, as one who serves by the strength that God supplies—in order that in everything God may be glorified through Jesus Christ. To Him belong glory and dominion forever and ever. Amen.*

> —1 Peter 4:10–11 ESV

The standard of ministry in the New Testament is not how it operates today. We are not as effective because we have veered from God's way. Too many ministers are looking for manifestations with a method so that they can call it their ministry. The last time I checked, it was the ministry of the Holy Spirit—the ministry of Jesus through us—not our ministry. If we are going to speak, we must speak by the Spirit. We must also address the enemy like the Spirit of God would address demons.

We are not supposed to focus on the fact that demons obey us; our focus should be on our salvation and that we are ambassadors.

The Lord in our midst is a victorious warrior; He has defeated the enemy. The enemy obeys us only because of Jesus Christ, not us. That is why Jesus said not to rejoice when the enemy listens to you, but rejoice that your names are written in Heaven. Who wrote your name there? Jesus did. He wrote our names in the Lamb's Book of Life because He purchased us long ago (1 Corinthians 6:20). Demons obey us solely for this reason, not because we are spiritual or to be feared. The enemy knows who we are but obeys us only because we are associated with Jesus Christ. We all must remember this.

ANGELS WAR ON OUR BEHALF

Bless the Lord, you His angels, who excel in strength, who do His word, heeding the voice of His word.

—Psalm 103:20

> **The enemy knows who we are but obeys us only because we are associated with Jesus Christ.**

Sometimes, when angels show up, we can step into a new place, just like what happened with Joshua. Joshua was moving into new territory when he met the captain of the Lord's army and did not even discern that it was an angel. At first, he thought a human being was confronting him. The angel was not taking sides but following the Lord's instruction. Angels encamp around us and do the Lord's bidding, hearkening unto His voice. Their arrival sometimes causes instant deliverance.

The enemy might be routed due to angelic activity, and you would not have an inkling of what happened; you would not be able to explain it or create a seminar. All you would know is that the enemy's eyes suddenly got big, and he ran off.

We would never want to take credit for this because the Lord Jesus Christ sends angels to surround us, which results in deliverance. Although I often witness angelic activity, I want to see more of it in all our lives. God intervenes in ways far too wonderful for it to ever come from us.

> *The angel of the Lord encamps around those who fear Him, and delivers them.*
>
> —Psalm 34:7

The angel encamps around the people who fear the Lord. So that is your job—to fear the Lord—and the angel gets the credit for encamping around you. You hardly hear any teaching about the fear of the Lord; however, the fear of the Lord brings in the angel to deliver you.

Psalm 34:7 mentions one singular angel, just as the captain of the host of the Lord's army was just one being in Joshua 5:13–15. He was the head commander of the angelic host of Heaven. The captain of the Lord's army may even be Jesus Himself, which is what I believe. This was implied when I was in Heaven, although I was not explicitly shown it was Him. The Bible does not specify whether the captain of the host is Jesus, but I felt that He was when I was there. Always remember that the angel of the Lord encamps around those who fear Him.

> *And he answered, Fear not: for they that be with us are more than they that be with them.*
>
> —2 Kings 6:16 KJV

These military angels are sent to encompass you and are ministering spirits sent forth to minister for those who are going to inherit salvation (Hebrews 1:14). When I was in Heaven, Jesus shared a very profound statement with me: Everyone was purchased—not one human being was not redeemed through His blood. Everyone was destined by God, who wrote their books and planned for them to come to the knowledge of Jesus Christ.

However, most people on earth do not understand their destiny. Even though the price was paid and the angels were sent to minister to people destined to inherit salvation, many still reject the Lord and go to hell. Yet their books are written as though they go to Heaven. The angels do not take sides with individuals; they only do the will of the Father.

Jesus showed me that angels were sent to unsaved people to bring them to a place of the knowledge of God. They lead them to a place where people preach the gospel and mentor them, hoping they get saved. These angels are sent to minister for those who will inherit salvation (Hebrews 1:14)—it is preemptive, on credit. In other words, before people are saved, the angels are told to minister to them. They are to lead them to situations where they can encounter the truth. For example, an angel may bring someone in your path so that you can talk to them or that God can meet their need, providing through you.

> *Jesus said to him, "I am the way, the truth, and the life. No one comes to the Father except through Me."*
>
> —John 14:6

God keeps unsaved people safe from all kinds of situations where they would have died before they accept salvation; this is the truth. Jesus said that He treats people like they are coming to Heaven; the angels are also instructed that way. This truth is not widely accepted, but the Lord sees everyone as coming to be with Him because He purchased all humanity. That means that everyone has the chance to accept Jesus Christ. If they accept Him as the way, they enter the Kingdom of God; if not, they will not.

INSTANT DELIVERANCE

And the God of peace shall bruise satan under your feet shortly. The grace of our Lord Jesus Christ be with you. Amen.

—Romans 16:20 KJV

Luke 10:19 talks about believers trampling on serpents and scorpions, having power and authority over all the enemy. In Romans 16:20, Paul specifically mentioned that satan would shortly be bruised under the feet of the Roman congregation that he addressed in this letter. God gave Paul that word for them. We address the enemy the same way today. We must believe that no matter what harassment we are going through with the enemy, it is just a matter of time before we crush satan under our feet—this word is for us too.

Thou art my hiding place; Thou shalt preserve me from trouble; Thou shalt compass me about with songs of deliverance. Selah.

—Psalm 32:7 KJV

Psalm 32:7 promises that we are preserved because God provides a hiding place to protect us from trouble. God gives us a fortress, a hiding place, that we can run to that will keep us from danger.

Just like He promised in Zephaniah 3:17, He will surround you, encompassing you with songs of deliverance. God Himself will sing over you. I have awakened at night and heard the Lord singing songs of deliverance over me. Because of the Lord's protection through these songs, the enemy could not operate against me or even touch me. Eventually, the hiding place became permanent; the Lord wants to do this for you too. This promise is not just for me; it is in the Bible and available to everybody.

We all can take the words of the Bible as our own. We must expect the Lord to provide that hiding place for us, mentioned in Psalm 32:7, and instruct us how to get there. Once we are in there, we're preserved from trouble, period. That would be enough for me, but He adds that He will encompass us. When God sings these songs about deliverance over and around us, the enemy will leave us because the Lord is essentially prophesying over us. When He speaks, it is a done deal; the enemy knows that. When God surrounds us this way, there is instant deliverance.

My question is, with what has been offered to us in the Scriptures, why do we depend so much on alternatives for our deliverance? God has offered us so much help and so many benefits. We settle for counterfeits because we don't know the truth. I used to seek others out to pray over me for deliverance and to deal with the devil; in some instances, it helped, yet I noticed it was not permanent. It was temporary because the truth had not become a part of me. The reality of my deliverance had not been fortified with the Word of God.

To maintain my deliverance, I learned that I needed to fill my house with the Word of God so that my spiritual being grew more powerful. The Lord once showed me how big my inner man was in the spirit; I was much bigger, like a giant, in the spirit in comparison to my body.

Back when I was in the operating room and the Lord appeared to me and took me to Heaven, He showed me that I had developed my spiritual walk with Him so that the sphere of influence of my spirit reached a circumference of thirty feet if I stood in the middle.

Jesus also showed me the apostle Lester Sumrall, whose spiritual proximity was the size of the entire city of San Francisco. When brother Sumrall went there and to other cities, the demons would be arrested. To prevent being cast out, they intentionally left town before he arrived so they would not come under his authority. The demons thought that if they went on their own, when Brother Sumrall left the city, they would be able to return; however, if Jesus addressed them, they had to obey. The Lord showed me that when he came to the city of San Francisco, the evil spirits came under his authority and were paralyzed. His presence affected entire regions.

What did the Holy Spirit reveal to you regarding this chapter?

_____

_____

_____

_____

_____

_____

_____

_____

_____

_____

_____

_____

_____

_____

_____

_____

_____

_____

_____

_____

_____

_____

_____

CHAPTER 10

God Is Your Deliverer

*How God anointed Jesus of Nazareth with
the Holy Spirit and with power, who went
about doing good and healing all who were
oppressed by the devil, for God was with Him.*

—Acts 10:38

I want to note that the Holy Spirit is said to have led Jesus into the desert to be tempted by the devil. This leading sounds strange to many of us because of how we have been taught; it is contrary to the mindset that many of us have about God. Matthew 4:1–11 talks about the temptation of Jesus where the Holy Spirit actually set up a confrontation between Him and the devil.

JESUS IS OUR ULTIMATE EXAMPLE

Then Jesus was led up by the Spirit into the wilderness to be tempted by the devil.

—Matthew 4:1

Jesus was just obeying as He was led into the desert and went face-to-face with the devil. When satan addressed Him, Jesus did not respond as the Son of God; He responded as a servant sent by God and anointed by the Holy Spirit (Philippians 2:6–8). Jesus did this for us without needing to prove anything; God created helel, the angel who became corrupted that we now call satan. After the fall, he came to be known as lucifer, the god of this world who stole the human race from God through Adam and Eve.

Jesus had to combat with the devil as the Son of Man; He did not wage war as the Son of God. Acts 10:38 clearly expresses that He was Jesus of Nazareth, who was anointed by the Holy Spirit and went around doing good, healing everyone who was oppressed by the devil because God was with Him.

> *You must have the same attitude that Christ Jesus had. Though He was God, He did not think of equality with God as something to cling to. Instead, He gave up His divine privileges; He took the humble position of a slave and was born as a human being. When He appeared in human form, He humbled Himself in obedience to God and died a criminal's death on a cross. Therefore, God elevated Him to the place of highest honor and gave Him the name above all other names.*
>
> —Philippians 2:5–9 NLT

Jesus went into the desert as a human being; He was God in a body but lived as a servant. The Scriptures say in Philippians 2:6–7 that He laid aside His Godhead ability, considering equality with God as nothing. Jesus did not operate as a deity but as one who serves. He lived and ministered as the anointed Person called the Son of Man, which is controversial yet true.

When Jesus encountered demons, they recognized Him and said, "You are the Son of God." He told them to shut up because He wanted to be known as the Son of Man. When He was in the desert, satan confronted Him as the Son of God; however, Jesus responded as the Son of Man. Satan tempted Jesus to try to get Him to operate as the Son of God, which He was not allowed to do.

> *I tell you the truth, anyone who believes in Me will do the same works I have done, and even greater works, because I am going to be with the Father.*
>
> —John 14:12 NLT

Jesus lived on earth as a servant. After He was crucified and resurrected, He taught the disciples to live the same way, encouraging them that they would do even greater works because He was going to the Father (John 14:12). Jesus had to accomplish the Father's will as a human under the guidance, power, and anointing of the Holy Spirit so that He could transfer His ministry to His body, which is all of us on earth. God's plan was that

Jesus operated as the Son of Man, and satan knew it, so he tried to throw Him off track by saying, "If you are the Son of God, do this." In other words, he challenged Jesus by saying that if you really are who you claim to be, then prove it.

What satan asked Jesus to do in the wilderness was out of bounds of what He was permitted to do as a human, so He refused. He resisted the temptations to act as the Son of God by telling satan no and deferring to the Father. He replied to all three temptations, saying, "It is written" (Matthew 4:4, 7, 10). We are supposed to respond to the enemy just like Jesus did by deferring to the words that came out of God's mouth. Every time satan demanded a miracle, Jesus countered his words; He refused to jump off a building or turn a rock into bread. He would not give in to these temptations because satan was trying to get Him to operate out of God's boundaries. The bottom line is that we are to do the same; if Jesus used the Word of God to combat the devil, then that is what we need to do as well.

GOD'S WORD COMBATS THE ENEMY

This charge I commit unto thee, son Timothy, according to the prophecies which went before on thee, that thou by them mightiest war a good warfare.

—1 Timothy 1:18 KJV

In 1 Timothy 1:18, Paul reminded Timothy of the prophecies spoken over him. I believe Paul delivered those words before Timothy, meaning they were looking forward. These prophetic utterances had to do with his future. Paul instructed him to use them as weapons of warfare. We should take

If Jesus used the Word of God to combat the devil, then that is what we need to do as well.

prophecies as the word of the Lord and declare them in response to the enemy. You can establish the framework of what God is saying to you about your future by proclaiming forward-looking utterances; allow them to go before you. Use those weapons you've been given—prophetic words—to wage war against the enemy. Even if you have not received a prophetic message from someone, you should prophetically be using the Word of God to wage war on your own.

You do not need to pay somebody to train or deliver you; however, at times, you need help because you are so overwhelmed and have allowed the enemy to come in. That is where the body of Christ can help. Yet must you seek out a special minister for deliverance?

We do not see Paul charging for deliverance or even ministering it. He did not come to cast demons out of Timothy; he had already released a prophetic utterance, then instructed him to take those words and beat up the devil. Paul charged Timothy to start fighting with his prophecies. He did not need to lay hands on him, address the devil, break demonic powers, and all these methods that we think we need a deliverance minister to do. Paul essentially told Timothy, "You have the weapons [which were prophecies], just use them."

> Therefore I remind you to stir up the gift of God which is in you through the laying on of my hands.
>
> —2 Timothy 1:6

In this passage, Paul charged Timothy to stir up the gift he received by the laying on of hands and fan it into flame. In other words, it had gone out. What was once a fire became like hot coals; maybe it was smoking and had some heat, but he needed to fan it into flame.

The effectiveness of a spiritual gift or impartation has to do with how the individual stewards it. Timothy needed to take action. Again, the question is, "Did Timothy need another word?" No. He needed to take the words he already received and wage war with them—that was enough. It was the same with the giftings. How often do you need hands laid on you before you are satisfied with your gifting? Your gifting—everything you are meant to obtain in Christ—is inside you and predestined from the foundations of the world (Ephesians 1:4–6; Romans 11:29).

The plans for your life were written before you were born (Psalm 139:16). Salvation was already established before Jesus hung on the cross. Revelation 13:8 says that He was the Lamb slain before the foundations of the world. God already saw Him slain before He created the universe. All the good works you were created to do were predestined in Christ. Even though people still go to hell, they were supposed to do the good works written in their books. Nobody needs to go to hell, but people still do.

So much is written about you that has yet to be done. You should see how thick your book is and how little is done compared to the potential. In Heaven, Jesus showed me that I was operating at 35 percent, yet I had so much education and experience. I experienced multiple supernatural encounters, even before I went to Heaven. I attended the best ministerial schools and had almost every general that you can name lay hands on me. I sat under many great ministers, had their anointing come upon me in their meetings, and even received prophecies from some of them. Despite all that happened to me, I did not get past 35 percent of what I could have done; the deficit was 65 percent. I was only doing about one-third of what was written about me.

When I discovered how little I had done with what I had been given, I sincerely told Jesus I would have done so much more if I had known. Jesus said nothing to me, but the Holy Spirit said, "You could have known." I then knew it was my responsibility, and the conversation was over. If I said anything else, I would get myself in trouble because it was my fault, not God's.

You can sit there and tell the Trinity that life was hard and you had a lot of hard knocks. Although you may have experienced many disadvantages, your reward in Heaven is based only on what you were given. God is looking for you to produce a return on what He has placed in you.

> *But you are a chosen race, a royal priesthood, a holy nation, a people for His own possession, that you may proclaim the excellencies of Him who called you out of darkness into His marvelous light.*

> —1 Peter 2:9 ESV

We have all experienced a measure of deliverance because we were delivered from the kingdom of darkness into the kingdom of light. We used to obey this prince of the power of the air, but we no longer do because we now have the ability to resist him (Ephesians 2:1–3). When we were lost, we could not say no to satan, the god of this world; we were powerless and strictly obedient to him.

Deliverance means being rescued from spiritual darkness and experiencing salvation by being born again. That same resurrection power that rose Jesus from the dead delivered and translated you. You have already been transferred into God's kingdom of light.

A FILLED HOUSE KEEPS DEMONS OUT

If the enemy overcomes you in a particular circumstance, you may need somebody else to pray for you. However, when you always need other people to pray for you, you will not see permanent results. I understand that you can receive true deliverance from ministers.

My wife, Kathi, was permanently delivered by receiving ministry from an individual, but she did not seek it; she was just in the meeting and was called out by the gifts of the Spirit. She was already saved when this person addressed an evil spirit that was harassing her, and it never came back. Kathi filled herself with the Word of God, and that place was occupied by the Holy Spirit and the Word, which is why it was permanent.

> When an unclean spirit goes out of a man, he goes through dry places, seeking rest, and finds none. Then he says, "I will return to my house from which I came." And when he comes, he finds it empty, swept, and put in order. Then he goes out and takes with him seven other spirits more wicked than himself, and they enter and dwell there; and the last state of that man is

*worse than the first. So shall it also be with this
wicked generation.*

—Matthew 12:43–45

Concerning deliverance, Jesus taught that when you
cast out a demon, it leaves and goes to an arid, desert
place; this is difficult for the evil spirit because it wants to
return to where it lived. When that unclean spirit returns,
it finds the person swept clean, which is what sometimes
happens in deliverance. The key in Matthew 12:43–45 is
that the person was found empty or unoccupied.

The passage does not specify if the person had ever
been filled with the Holy Spirit; the bottom line was that
the evil spirit could come back if that individual was
not currently occupied with the Spirit and the Word
of God filling up their house. If they were empty, the
evil spirit would then find other disembodied spirits to
come back with it, leaving the person seven times worse
than their original condition.

You must remember that if you cast a devil out of a
person, they need to be discipled and mentored in the
Word of God and the Holy Spirit so that their house is
filled; that way, the evil spirit will not be able to return.
Being discipled and mentored in the Word of God is
the whole message behind what Jesus said in Matthew
12:43–45, where He made deliverance easy. Today,
most deliverance ministries focus on casting demons
out of people, yet they are not fathering or mentoring.
Fathering or mentoring may not go over well, but it is

not helping anybody just to cast the devil out. Based on what we see today, many have ignored Jesus's teaching.

My concern regarding deliverance ministry is not just what happens today, but the person's well-being tomorrow. In other words, if I address the devil in your life and drive him out, have I done the fathering and mentoring for you to maintain your freedom? Have I provided you with the tools to fill you up and allow the Holy Spirit to occupy you so completely that the evil spirit cannot return? Like Kathi, I want you to stay free. Most people end up worse off if they are not mentored and filled with the Holy Spirit and the Word of God. You must have the Scriptures in your arsenal to combat the enemy like Jesus did in Matthew 4; your deliverance must be sealed.

> *For the word of God is alive and powerful. It is sharper than the sharpest two-edged sword, cutting between soul and spirit, between joint and marrow. It exposes our innermost thoughts and desires.*
>
> —Hebrews 4:12 NLT

> *Above all, taking the shield of faith with which you will be able to quench all the fiery darts of the wicked one. And take the helmet of salvation, and the sword of the Spirit, which is the word of God.*
>
> —Ephesians 6:16–17

The word of God is a weapon—the sword of the Spirit—that cuts in, dividing between the soul and the spirit. When the enemy tries to come back or attack you, you must have the shield of faith; your faith must be built up to extinguish every lie from the enemy. Remember that you have all these tools; deliverance becomes very simple when you know how to use your weapons.

I am called to be a father, not just a teacher (1 Corinthians 4:15). The best way for me to father and mentor you is by sharing the truth through books and media; we have thousands and thousands of people, which makes it difficult to provide individual mentorship.

I want you to be in a class of warriors where you experience deliverance because the Lord comes to you and sings songs over you (Zephaniah 3:17). Wage war with the prophecies that have been given to you and fan your gifts into flame so that you do not have to depend on others (1 Timothy 1:18; 2 Timothy 1:6).

> **Deliverance becomes very simple when you know how to use your weapons.**

Even though the body of Christ is there for us, we should not focus on individuals for our answer. Paul essentially taught Timothy that everything he needed had been given to him; now he just had to fan it into flame and wage war with his prophecies.

He had to grow up. The bottom line is that every one of us has to mature at some point.

> *The righteous cry out, and the Lord hears, and delivers them out of all their troubles.*
>
> —Psalm 34:17

> *Then they cried out to the Lord in their trouble, and He delivered them out of their distresses.*
>
> —Psalm 107:6

> *Call upon Me in the day of trouble; I will deliver you, and you shall glorify Me.*
>
> —Psalm 50:15

Let us get back to the simplicity of deliverance. When you cry for help, the Lord hears and delivers you out of your trouble and distress; the Scriptures do not imply that it involves other individuals, even though we have each other. Psalm 50:15 says that you will call on the Lord in the day of trouble, and He will deliver you; you will glorify Him, not give credit to other people. God is your Deliverer. We need to get back to the basics.

You have been set on the path for permanent deliverance; then you will cause others to be set free, and it will last in their lives too. Why? Because you will disciple people, which leads to lasting breakthroughs. Through mentorship, they will be occupied by the truth and the Holy Spirit.

A PRAYER FOR YOU

Father, thank you for giving us the authority to drive out the enemy in the name of Jesus and through the power of His blood. Thank you for every reader receiving their deliverance as You sing songs over them and send Your angels to encamp around them. Thank you for the Messiah's anointing, permanently breaking the yokes off people. Lord, I pray that You also turn their testimonies into deliverance for others. I declare that they are Your ambassadors who carry deliverance with them. Father, confirm Your word with signs and wonders following, in the name of Jesus. Amen.

What did the Holy Spirit reveal to you regarding this chapter?

_____

_____

_____

_____

_____

_____

_____

_____

_____

_____

_____

_____

_____

_____

_____

_____

_____

_____

_____

_____

_____

_____

SALVATION PRAYER

Lord God,

I confess that I am a sinner.

I confess that I need Your Son, Jesus.

Please forgive me in His Name.

*Lord Jesus, I believe You died
for me and that You*

are alive and listening to me now.

I now turn from my sins and welcome

*You into my heart. Come and
take control of my life.*

*Make me the kind of person
You want me to be.*

Now, fill me with Your Holy Spirit,

who will show me how to live for You.

I acknowledge You before men

as my Savior and my Lord.

In Jesus's name. Amen.

IF YOU PRAYED THIS PRAYER,
PLEASE GET IN TOUCH WITH US AT

info@kevinzadai.com

We welcome you to join our network at
Warriornotes.tv for access to
exclusive programming.

To enroll in our ministry school, go to:
www.Warriornotesschool.com

Visit **www.KevinZadai.com** for
additional ministry materials.

ABOUT
DR. KEVIN ZADAI

Kevin Zadai, ThD, was called to the ministry at the age of ten. He attended Central Bible College in Springfield, Missouri, where he received a bachelor of arts in theology. Later, he received training in missions at Rhema Bible College and a ThD at Primus University. Dr. Kevin L. Zadai is dedicated to training Christians to live and operate in two realms simultaneously—the supernatural and the natural.

At age thirty-one, Kevin met Jesus in Heaven, got a second chance at life, and received a revelation that he could not fail because it is all rigged in our favor! Kevin holds a commercial pilot license and is retired from Southwest Airlines after twenty-nine years as a flight attendant. He is the founder and president of Warrior Notes School of Ministry. He and his lovely wife, Kathi, reside in New Orleans, Louisiana.

Check It Out!

Other Recent Books by Dr. Kevin Zadai

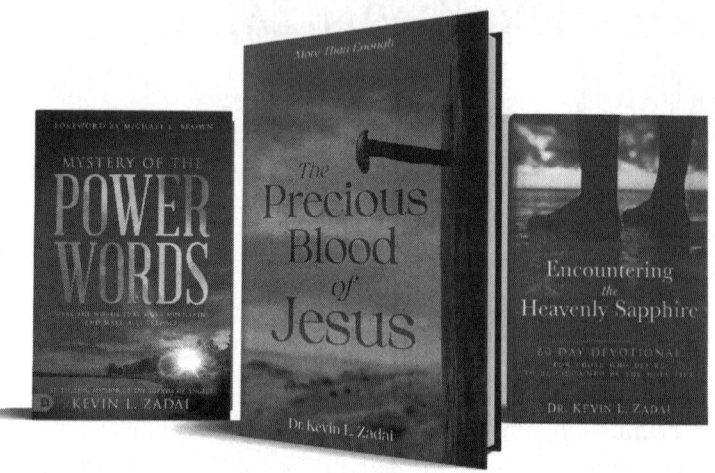

Mystery of the Power Words: Speak the Words That Move Mountains and Make Hell Tremble

The Precious Blood of Jesus

Encountering The Heavenly Sapphire: 60 Day Devotional for Those Who Desire to be Consumed by The Holy Fire

Kevin has written over sixty-five books and study guides.

Please see our website for a complete list of materials.

www.Kevinzadai.com